Monetary Policy and Rational Expectations

Monetary Policy and Rational Expectations

GEORGE MACESICH

PRAEGER

New York
Westport, Connecticut
London

Library of Congress Cataloging-in-Publication Data

Macesich, George, 1927–
   Monetary policy and rational expectations.

   Includes index.
   1. Monetary policy.   2. Rational expectations
(Economic theory)   I. Title.
HG230.3.M33   1987   332.4'6   86-20538
ISBN 0-275-92327-4 (alk. paper)

Library of Congress Catalog Card Number: 86-20538
ISBN: 0-275-92327-4

First published in 1987

Praeger Publishers, 521 Fifth Avenue, New York, NY 10175
A division of Greenwood Press, Inc.

Printed in the United States of America

∞

The paper used in this book complies with the Permanent
Paper Standard issued by the National Information Standards
Organization (Z39.48-1984).

10 9 8 7 6 5 4 3 2 1

Copyright Acknowledgments

We gratefully acknowledge permission to quote from the following sources:

Milton Friedman, "Leon Walras and His Economic System," *American Economic Review*, December 1955. By permission of the author and the American Economic Association.

Milton Friedman, "Monetary Policy: Theory and Practice," *Journal of Money, Credit, and Banking*, February 1982. By permission of the Ohio State University Press.

To
W. M., Sr., and Jr.

Contents

viii   Contents

Preface

This study deals with the importance of expectations in the formulation and execution of monetary policy. It draws on monetary theory, the experiences of several countries in the post-World War II period, and the on-going debate over monetary policy and monetary regimes.

The importance of significant time lags between the initiation of monetary policy and the effects of these changes on the economy has long been recognized by economists. This view is now in dispute by an important segment of the economics profession. The new classical economists stress the important role that rational expectations have in economic policy and in determining economic activity, prices, interest rates, and employment. In effect, decisions regarding the economy depend crucially on expectations regarding future government policies. Even though their policy prescriptions are similar to the monetarists, they differ from the monetarists in fundamental approach.

This book is directed to the general economist (rather than specifically to the specialist), to students of economics, and to laymen. I am indebted to many colleagues and friends with whom I have discussed one aspect or another of this study over the years. These include Munir Choudhary, Milton Friedman, Anna J. Schwartz, Marshal R. Colberg, and Walter Macesich, Jr. I would also like to express appreciation to Chrys Ivey Biederman for efficient and helpful typing services.

Monetary Policy
and
Rational Expectations

CHAPTER 1

Debate over Monetary Policy

THE ISSUES

Myth, fact, and fancy dominate attempts to formulate and execute monetary policy both domestically and internationally. Monetary policy is placed high on the agenda in international conferences. It is one of the key issues that plague architects of government policy.

Basic questions regarding monetary policy, including the relations between debtor and creditor countries and their respective responsibilities in the international adjustment process, all come up for discussion if not resolution. The various solutions advanced always come encumbered with their heavy economic, political, and ideological baggage. This leaves the puzzling choice between real and spurious solutions. The net effect is that few problems can ever have been so ingeniously contrived to maximize difficulty as that of the formulation and execution of monetary policy on both the domestic and international levels.

It is argued that monetary policy influences primarily the value and composition of assets. As a consequence, it is more circuitous than, for example, fiscal policy, which directly influences income and therefore economic activity. A contrary position is the argument that a decision regarding the demand to hold money really involves a decision as to whether it is best to hold wealth in this form or in securities or physical assets. Against such a background, asset holdings may be as income in directly influencing economic activity. Through its effect upon assets, monetary policy theoretically may have as direct an impact on economic activity as fiscal policy operating through income. The empirical evidence tends to support this view.

Prior to the 1930s theoretical and empirical research in monetary theory and policy focused on the institutional determinants of velocity. Since that time considerable attention has been given to the relation between velocity, or its alternative formulation—the demand for money, and interest rates. The possible existence of the Keynesian liquidity trap and the consequent ineffectiveness of monetary policy probably motivated much of this research. In themselves many of these studies left much to be desired. To judge from results reported elsewhere, the demand for cash balances does in fact depend partly on interest rates.

Though opinions differ, evidence does suggest that, in general, monetary authority can control nominal quantities and direct the quantity of its own liabilities. By manipulating the quantity of its own liabilities it can fix the exchange rate, the price levels, the nominal level of material income, and the nominal quantity of money; it also has a direct influence on the rate of inflation or deflation, the rate of growth of the nominal stock of money, and the rate of growth or decline in nominal material income. Again, though opinions differ, the bulk tends to tilt on the side that the monetary authority cannot through control of nominal quantities fix real quantities such as the real interest rate, the rate of unemployment, the level of real national income, the real quantity of money, the rate of growth of real material income, or the rate of growth of real quantity of money.

Economists are quick to point out, however, that this does not mean that monetary policy does not have important effects on these real magnitudes. Indeed, when money gets out of order, important repercussions are felt throughout the economy. Monetary history provides evidence on this point.

The debate continues as strong as ever over the effectiveness of monetary policy as a means for influencing economic activity. Keynesians over the years have argued that money and monetary policy have little or no impact on income and employment, particularly during severe economic depressions. Moreover, government taxation and spending, in effect fiscal policy, are most effective when dealing with problems of inflation and unemployment.

Monetarists stress the importance of money. They argue that a rule that requires the monetary authority to cause the nominal stock of money to increase by an annual fixed percentage would effectively reduce fluctuations in prices, real output, and employment.

More recently, the new classical economists argue that adjustment in the nominal variables, such as nominal income prices, is complete and expectations are rational in the short run. They differ from monetarist and Keynesian views on this point. The importance of this difference is that to monetarists and Keynesians a government's demand management policies exercised through monetary policy and fiscal policy can be effective means for stabilizing the economy. Anticipated government demand management policies, according to the new classicals, will leave no effect. There are no trade-offs, for instance, between employment and inflation even in the short run. The effect of anticipated demand management policies of government is only inflation. On the other hand, such policies can be used to solve the problem of inflation without undue loss of real output.

This study focuses on the issues cast up by the on-going debate between monetarists, Keynesians, and new classicals over monetary policy as a means for influencing economic activity. The merits of the debate and positions taken are considered against the experiences of several developed and developing countries. The remainder of this chapter discusses briefly the background to the debate over monetary policy, monetary targets, and monetary authorities.

BACKGROUND TO THE DEBATE

Keynes's idea expressed in his book *General Theory* provided the basis of post-World War II economic policy including monetary policy for the United States and other Western industrial nations. Basic to Keynesian doctrine is the use of government fiscal power to stimulate the economy when unemployment is high and to restrain the economy when high employment and excessive demand begin to cause wage and price rises to reach an inflationary rate.

In general, postwar economic and monetary policies have been post-Keynesian in the sense that most theorists and policymakers in major Western countries have agreed in principle on Keynesian ideas of how to deal with unemployment and inflation. Since their triumph in the postwar period, Keynesian policies have not always come up to expectations.

A number of factors appear to have influenced their outcome. The inflationary outburst in the mid-1960s appears to be traceable to the cold war and its hot manifestation, the Vietnam War. Fiscal mismanagement by the federal government and new Great Society programs added to the pressures. The United States was flawed for contributing to European inflation by forcing overvalued dollars on the Europeans, particularly in the form of investment. In the decade of the 1970s, crop failures and soaring oil prices compounded world problems.

When President Kennedy took office in 1961, the level of output was below capacity, and unemployment for the previous three years had been around 6 percent and was rising. New Frontier economists diagnosed the trouble as stemming from the Eisenhower administration's overrestrictive fiscal policy. In the previous two years, the federal budget had shown an approximate balance despite the 1958–1959 recession.

The Kennedy administration set a "full employment" target of 4 percent unemployment and set out to stimulate the economy by increasing federal spending and sending the budget into deficit. Monetary policy was "easy" and interest rates were kept "low." These expansive measures were reinforced by the tax cut granted in 1964. Wage and price guidelines were pressed into service in an attempt to keep the economy on an even keel.

When the economic situation began to get out of hand in 1965, Keynesians urged fiscal measures in the form of tax increases. On account of the escalating Vietnam War and Great Society costs that were either underestimated or understated and an unwillingness to take action for fear of inviting public criticism, President Johnson rejected the advice of his own economic advisors. Fiscal measures were not implemented. The resulting huge budget deficits served to escalate inflation.

One can argue, of course, that Keynesian economics did not fail. Political leadership in fact mismanaged the economy and brought the country to the brink of disaster. Keynes always assumed that a capable and sophisticated political leadership would be at hand to administer and manage the affairs of nations. This does not always happen. Economic theory often gives way to political reality.

Affairs were not much better served by President Nixon's administration. In early 1969 a tax surcharge tardily voted by Congress, together with administration efforts to counter inflation with a combination of tighter fiscal and monetary policies, attempted to achieve a return to full employment and price stability. This is now the familiar policy of "gradualism," which failed to control inflation. The policy might have been more successful if the dollar had not "weakened" in the summer of 1971 with the closing of the gold window.

As a result, stricter measures were put in place. These measures included wage and price controls and were labeled the New Economic Policy (NEP). The net effect of NEP anti-inflation policies appears to have been the raising of interest rates by the Federal Reserve System. It was expected that monetarism would be tried by the Nixon administration, but this did not happen. In fact, President Nixon's administration opted for the Keynesian concept of the "full employment budget." Accordingly, monetary policy and fiscal policy were to be used to stimulate the economy when unemployment rose above 4 percent and measures were to be taken to restrain the economy when the full employment goal was reached. Just how Keynesian the administration was becoming is suggested by the 1975 budget, when the administration was willing to consider a major program of public service employment if unemployment reached "serious" proportions.

In retrospect, the evidence does suggest that for more than a quarter-century after World War II discretionary monetary and fiscal policies have had a mixed record in reducing cyclical fluctuations that were indeed mild by historical standards.[1] By the 1970s these discretionary policies oscillated between attempts to combat inflation and attempts to combat unemployment, with poor timing and, for the most part, indifferent and perverse results. In effect, the turbulent 1970s were dominated by discretionary policies and seemingly uncontrollable inflation, recessions, sharp declines in real wages, unemployment, energy problems, as well as various raw material shortages. They stand in marked contrast to the comparatively prosperous early postwar years, which appeared to justify the optimism of Keynesians and their reform liberal allies.

The "stagflationary" disappointments of the 1970s, the high rates of unemployment, inflation, and interest, the depressed stock market, the slowdowns in productivity and growth and capital formation discredited Keynesianism and its intellectually reformed liberalism and ushered in a political and ideological counterrevolution spearheaded by monetarism and neoliberalism in the form of "Reaganomics" in the United States and "Thatcherism" in Great Britain.

Just as Keynesian theory inspired the revolution, so a wave of professional reaction to the synthesis of Keynesian and neoclassical doctrines that became orthodox in the 1950s and 1960s sustains the counterrevolution. I have discussed elsewhere the important intellectual role of Milton Friedman, the monetarists, and the Chicago School in bringing the counterrevolution.[2] Suffice it to say here, the doctrines of Keynes and reform liberalism considered new at the turn of the century and into the Depression are discredited, and now challenged, by the doctrines of neo-liberalism and monetarism of more than a hundred years ago. These doctrines now appear to be guiding philosophies of Congress, Parliament, president, and prime minister. To be sure, there are many divergencies in economic theory, popular ideology, and actual policy. Nonetheless, the counterrevolution has compelled a debate on the economic assumption of the last two generations. It has at the same time questioned the growth of government power and intervention in economic and political affairs.

MONETARY TARGETS AND MONETARY AUTHORITIES

I have discussed elsewhere the issue of means and ends in several countries regarding the methods of monetary control.[3] How can a central bank control monetary growth? One approach is through interest rates. The other is by controlling the monetary base directly. Interest rates affect the demand for money as suggested elsewhere;[4] but the interest rate effects may be overwhelmed by other effects. This suggests that the central bank is better advised to operate more directly on the supply through the monetary base. These magnitudes can be controlled. As a result, monetary growth can be affected in more predictable ways than through interest rates.

Monetarist preference for a "monetary aggregate target" rather than a "money market target" as the appropriate target for monetary policy is closely associated with their view of the control of nominal and real rates of interest.[5] As we discussed earlier, monetarists hold that the authorities are at best able to fix the nominal rate of interest. Their theory on the real rate of interest emphasizes the importance between the nominal market rate of interest and the real rate of interest. Only if the expected rate of inflation is equal will nominal and real rates of interest be zero.

The choice of an indicator that will quickly and accurately give the direction and magnitude of monetary policy is also closely associated with the monetarist preference for a "monetary aggregate target." A useful indicator must possess such characteristics as a high degree of correlation with the target variables, accurate and reliable statistics on the indicator quickly available to authorities, and exogeny rather than endogeny—monetary authorities should be capable of controlling the variable. Indeed, Anna J. Schwartz eliminates the distinction between targets and variables.[6]

In fact, the ideal target, Schwartz argues, ought to be judged on three criteria: (1) Is it measurable? (2) Is it subject to control by central banks? (3) Is it a reliable indicator of monetary conditions? On the basis of data for the United Kingdom, Canada, and Japan, Schwartz concludes that the money stock is the best "target-indicator." Similar conclusions are suggested in other studies.

I have presented results elsewhere suggesting that central banks only rarely succeed in hitting monetary targets.[7] When they miss, it is nearly always in overshooting, creating "base-drift." The base-drift problem occurs if the supply of money ends up above its ceiling, raising the issue of what should be used as the starting point for the next target. By unsettling financial markets, base-drift creates additional difficulties for the monetary authority in its effort to achieve longer-term monetary goals.

How seriously, then, should governments react to such sequels? If the monetary target is a single measure, there is little choice with which to judge policy. In low-inflation countries—Japan, Switzerland, West Germany—this would not seem to be a problem. Their narrow and broad definitions of money have been moving closely in line with each other. When they decide to change target rates, the choice is clear. The United States uses several target definitions to assure itself that a broad thrust to policy is correct. If all targets are missed, then clearly something is wrong and presumably something else is required.

Our discussion of the new classicals and their emphasis on equilibrium and rational expectations theory suggests at least one reason for the lack of better performance in target practice on the part of central banks. Another is the public's diminished credibility in the monetary authorities and the central bank to behave in a consistent way. For these reasons, among others, monetary authorities are urged to abandon short-term stabilization attempts altogether and to pursue instead a credible long-term steady-state policy. One such policy is a constant money growth rule proposed by Milton Friedman and the monetarists. It is an idea that has been widely discussed for years.

Evidence also suggests why central banks have not adopted a "fixed monetary rule." It may well be, as some economists argue, including this writer, that discretionary policies serve the established bureaucracies. Such a policy permits them to take credit when economic conditions are good and allow for disclaimers of responsibility when economic conditions deteriorate.

Another reason for such reluctance may be in the degree of "independence" possessed by central banks. Such independence depends on (1) the method of appointment of governors; (2) the length of time they serve; (3) whether they have legislated objectives clear enough to be a barrier to government intervention; and (4) whether their constituencies provide the bank or the government with final authority for monetary policy. In practice, central banks may have rather less or rather more freedom than charters suggest. This is likely to depend on tradition as well as on the personalities involved.

Only the German Bundesbank has final authority for monetary policy. The governor, moreover, is not directly appointed by the government. The National Bank of Yugoslavia is an independent federal institution established by federal law.[8] The bank is managed by the governor, who is appointed by the Federal Assembly on the recomendation of the Federal Executive Council. He is responsible to both of these institutions for the implementation of bank operations and targets. The Federal Assembly and the Federal Executive Council decide monetary policy targets, and the National Bank is responsible only for their implementation. In policy formation the National Bank, nonetheless, plays a significant if not dominant role in monetary policy, thanks to the ready acceptance of its proposals by policy makers.[9]

The central bank of the Netherlands has a clearly defined objective of price stability built into its constitution. On no other score could it be considered independent. In fact, the world's two oldest central banks, Riksbank of Sweden (1668) and the Bank of England (1694), are clearly subservient to their governments in the formation of monetary policy. In the United States and Germany, central bank control rests with a board composed of the heads of the several regional banks, thereby allowing for greater "independence" from the central government.

It is not surprising that central banks find themselves in the uncomfortable position where monetary and fiscal policies meet. They must meet the requirements of their governments. This means ensuring that the government is able to function smoothly in meeting its financial obligations. In many countries, government borrowing in the 1970s and 1980s has resulted in regular deficits and debt has risen as a proportion of gross national product.

Concern with inflation calls attention to the growth in the money supply. Governments have reacted by setting formal targets for monetary growth. Since central banks now try to achieve monetary targets while at the same time ostensibly financing much larger public-sector borrowing, their job is made all the more difficult. Their lack of enthusiasm in embracing monetarism is understandable. Such an embrace would impose severe constraints on the exercise of discretionary monetary authority. On the other hand, a clearly defined policy of rules would rescind central banks from the political quagmire in which they now find themselves stuck while in pursuit of illusory goals.

NOTES

1. For a summary of a number of these issues see, for instance, George Macesich, *The Politics of Monetarism: Its Historical and Institutional Development* (Totowa, N.J.: Rowman and Allanheld, 1984).
2. Ibid.
3. Ibid.
4. George Macesich, *Monetarism: Theory and Policy* (New York: Praeger, 1983).
5. Ibid., p. 101.
6. Anna J. Schwartz, "Short-Term Targets of Three Foreign Central Banks," in *Targets and Indicators of Monetary Policy*, Karl Brunner, ed. (San Francisco: Chandler, 1969), pp. 20-25.
7. Ibid.

8. Macesich, *The Politics of Monetarism*, p. 102.

9. Dimitrije Dimitrijević and George Macesich, *Money and Finance in Yugoslavia: A Comparative Analysis* (New York: Praeger, 1984).

CHAPTER 2

In Search of a Monetary Regime: The International Dimension

A BRETTON WOODS II?

On the subject of international monetary policy there is a simmering debate on calling a Bretton Woods II conference to consider, among other issues, what changes in the world's monetary system can be made to ease the problems of international adjustment, including the global debt problem. Should the world try to revive the fixed exchange system; or should it possibly return to a gold standard?

To some the idea of a Bretton Woods II conference is tempting to return to the serenity of a system of fixed exchange rates. To others a second Bretton Woods conference would be a nightmare. At the 1944 conference, only 44 countries were represented; today a truly global monetary conference would require invitations to 162 countries, with many clamoring for an equal vote with the major industrial nations.

The current system of floating exchange rates (or "dirty float") has plenty of critics. They argue that short-term fluctuations often lead to longer-term misalignments of currencies, making U.S. goods more expensive and less competitive abroad. As a result, the critics contend, businesses tend to shun export markets, world trade is depressed, and the debt problems of the poorer countries grow worse.

Memories on some matters tend to be short, for it is not at all clear that a system of fixed exchange rates would operate any better under current world conditions characterized by widely varying inflation rates and heavy international capital flows. As a matter of fact, the Bretton Woods system of fixed exchange rates worked for less than a decade. It really came into full operation in 1958 when the major European countries finally agreed to make their currency freely convertible into dollars. It began to fall apart in the late 1960s when the British pound came under heavy pressure as a consequence of internal economic difficulties. Moreover, frequent crises dominated the system as governments sought to defend unrealistic exchange rates. These contests, moreover, were generally won by the markets and lost by central banks. Before we turn to a discussion of the combination of circumstances that brought about the collapse of the Bretton Woods agreement, it is useful to consider briefly how in fact the agreement was brought about in the first place. Some accords are imperfect—such is the nature of compromise and human affairs generally. Some are lucky rather than skillful achievements— such are the happy contingencies of diplomacy. The Bretton Woods agreement is an excellent illustration of both elements.

Keynes's report after the 1944 Bretton Woods conference to the British Parliament explaining the nature and scope of the new international monetary system and its centerpiece, the International Monetary Fund (IMF), argues that the domestic supply of money would no longer be regulated by gold flows and the IMF proposals were the exact opposite of the gold standard.[1] Keynes's view was not shared by the Americans. In fact, the U.S. Congress was being presented with the view that the dollar was "defined" in terms of gold and that the IMF would operate much like the gold standard.

In Keynes's view, the new international order was "far removed from the old orthodoxy. If [IMF and Bretton Woods] agreements do so in terms as inoffensive as possible to the former faith, need we complain?"[2] All of this, he argued, serves to provide an international framework for the new ideas and new techniques associated with the domestic policy of full employment.

American proposals, at least initially, did not envision such drastic departure from orthodoxy nor that the United States was to be the principal stabilizer and in fact financially and economically underwrite the entire arrangement. Indeed, the initial American plan for an International Stabilization Fund, presented by Harry Dexter White, differed in three main points from the British plan for an International Clearing Union presented by Lord Keynes. In the first instance, the Americans opposed the creation of $26 billion in international liquidity that the British argued would be necessary to finance expansion of world trade and postwar recovery. They viewed such provisions for an increase in international liquidity as an application of the deficit financing translated from the domestic to the international scene and hence not likely to serve as a means for stabilization. Instead of new international reserves, the Americans proposed that the Stabilization Fund could just as well operate with a much smaller amount of $5 billion in gold and national currencies.

In the second instance, the Americans did not view with enthusiasm the proposal contained in the British plan for flexibility in exchange rates. They argued that exchange rates be fixed and changed only with the consent of 80 percent of the voting power. Finally, the Americans were not at all attracted to the British idea that pressure should be exerted in a creditor country to facilitate international adjustments. The Americans clearly expected to be the largest creditor in the postwar period and thus wished to limit American liability.

One other plan that never made the Bretton Woods agenda was the so-called key currency plan promoted by J. H. Williams of Harvard University and the Federal Reserve Bank of New York. It is worth noting, if only because what is strictly academic today might well be tomorrow's reality. The essence of Williams' proposal is that postwar stability really rested in the position of the American dollar and the British pound. They are the key currencies in the sense that they play dominant roles in the world trade, finance, and foreign exchange markets. According to Williams, internal monetary stability and cooperation between the United States and Great Britain is the critical issue and what happens to their currencies determines events in the rest of the world as well. If stability could be maintained in these two countries and in the dollar-pound exchange rate, stability in other countries would not present major difficulties.

A RETURN TO GOLD?

Europeans and particularly the French tended to opt for the gold standard and its advantages, which alternative systems do not possess—at least as practical worldwide systems. F. A. Hayek draws attention to at least three virtues of the gold standard that in view of postwar experience have consider-able merit to many people.[3] Although far from perfect, the gold standard did create an international currency without submitting domestic monetary policy to the decision of an in-ternational monetary authority. It did make monetary policy by and large automatic and fairly predictable. It did secure changes in the basic money that tended to be in the right di-rection. Moreover, the "ruling superstitious prejudice in favor of gold" made the international gold standard possible. Indeed this prejudice in favor of gold made an international money possible at a time when any other arrangements by interna-tional agreement and cooperation were unlikely.

Attempts to return to the gold standard as a constraint on the domestic and international monetary system have not met with notable success.[4] This is not surprising. What is often lacking in these proposals is an appreciation and understand-ing of the fact that the gold standard was more than a mone-tary standard. It cannot be understood, as it cannot be oper-ated successfully, except as part of a socioeconomic, political, and philosophic system in which it was developed. This sys-tem no longer exists.

There is, moreover, a tendency on the part of some gold ad-vocates to idealize the gold standard and overlook some of its more troublesome aspects. Thus between 1815 and 1914 there were 12 major crises or panics in the United States that pushed up interest rates, created severe unemployment, and sus-pended specie payments (conversion of dollars into gold), in addition to 14 minor recessions. To be sure, between 1879 and

1965—a period when the United States was on some sort of gold standard (the dollar's final links with gold were not cut until 1971 during President Nixon's administration)—the consumer price index rose by an average of only 1.4 percent a year. On the other hand, the severe bouts of inflation were followed by deep deflation in which prices actually fell. For instance, in the 1921 world recession, when production actually fell for only a few months, there were 20-40 percent cuts in manufacturing wages in some countries in the period 1920–1922.

Indeed, Keynes (1883–1946) and other critics were quick to point out that the international gold standard does not provide the world with the appropriate quantity of money to ensure price stability—though arrangements could be provided to compensate for the drawback.[5] Second, and perhaps more important, Keynes argued that wages tend "to rise beyond the limits set by the volume of money, but can only be prevented from doing so by the weapon of creating unemployment. This weapon the world after a good try, has decided to discard." To Keynes, the priority view of an international currency arrangement should be

to prevent not only those evils which result from a chronic shortage of international money due to the drawing of gold into creditor countries but also those which follow from countries failing to maintain stability of domestic efficiency costs and moving out of step with one another in their national wage policies and so different prices impossible under a strict gold standard.[6]

The error of the gold standard, according to Keynes, lay in "submitting national wage-policies to outside dictation. It is wiser to regard stability (or otherwise) of internal prices as a matter of internal policy and politics."

Some countries will be more successful than others in their pursuit of wage and price stability. As a portent of things to come in the postwar period, Keynes went on to observe that

some people argue that a capitalistic country is doomed to failure because it will be found impossible in conditions of full employment to prevent a progressive increase in wages. According to this view severe slumps and recurrent periods of unemployment have been hitherto the only effective means of holding efficiency wages within a reasonably stable range. Whether this is so remains to be seen. The more conscious we are of this problem, the likelier shall we be to surmount it.[7]

Not everyone agrees with Keynes' interpretation of prewar experience.

Hayek, for instance, in discussing lessons to be drawn from British prewar experience, argues that it was unique and exceptional in that the problem of unemployment was

largely a problem of a too-high *level* of real wages, and in which the much more crucial and general problem of flexibility of the wage *structure* could be neglected. As a result of Britain's return to gold in 1925 at the 1914 parity, a situation had been created in which it could be plausibly argued that all real wages in Britain had become too high for her to achieve the necessary volume of exports. I doubt whether the same has ever been true of any important country, and even whether it was entirely true of Britain in the 1920s. But of course Britain then had the oldest, most firmly entrenched and most comprehensive trade union movement in the world, which by its wage policy had succeeded in establishing a wage structure determined much more by considerations of justice, which meant little else than the preservation of traditional wage differentials, and which made those changes in relative wages demanded by an adaptation to changed conditions "politically impossible."[8]

It may well be that in the design of the postwar monetary system an important prewar lesson from British experience has not been incorporated. This is the lesson on the role of changes in relative wage rates and prices, reallocating labor and resources between industries so as to facilitate continuous adaptation to changing economic and technological conditions to maintain and advance real income and wealth. The substitutions of unions and other institutional arrangements for the market mechanism in setting wages and prices has become an established fact in many countries since World War II. The consequent wage and price rigidities viewed by many economists as now irreversible, requiring policies to be adapted accordingly, have imparted a severe inflationary bias to the world economy. Moreover, government macroeconomic policies designed to promote maximum employment and output serve in part to reinforce this inflationary bias.

The end product of American and British consultations, meetings, conferences, and redrafts of the Keynes and White plans over the period 1941–1944 was the Bretton Woods conference convened in July 1944 and the establishment of the International Monetary Fund. The operation of the IMF and the role of such reserve currencies as the dollar and pound shaped the postwar international monetary system.

COLLAPSE OF BRETTON WOODS I

By the mid-1960s, if not earlier, the Bretton Woods system began to show itself incapable of handling a very different world from that envisioned by its framers. Depending on one's viewpoint, it can be argued that the Bretton Woods system, thanks in large measure to American participation and generosity, enabled Europe and Japan to recover from the devastation of the war and established a stable monetary system as well as a more open trade and financial system that led to a period of unparalleled economic growth.

This was not to last. Partly because the system had become dollar-centered, persistent U.S. deficits and piling up of short-term indebtedness made it unlikely that the United States could honor its commitment to redeem dollar holdings of gold. Indeed, by the early 1960s Robert Triffin in his various writings noted that other countries derived from net American losses nearly 60 percent of their total reserve increases in the 1958–1962 period.[9]

This was simply not a safe and rational way to regulate the increase in international reserves that are to serve as an ultimate basis, especially under conditions of convertibility, for increases in national money supplies necessary to support growth levels of production and trade in an expanding world economy.

The postwar Bretton Woods system came to an end on August 15, 1971, when President Nixon announced his New Economic Policy, whereby the dollar would no longer be convertible into gold and a 10 percent surcharge would be imposed on dutiable imports. The "unthinkable," which so often dogs monetary history, occurred. The history of the international monetary system since that date has been one of the attempts to reimpose an "order" on the system.

There are no shortages of proposals for international monetary reform. Every economist eager to take his or her place in the history of monetary thought rushed forward with individual proposals. In addition to various versions of the dusted-off White and Keynes plans, we have also a Triffin Plan, a Stamp Plan, a Machlup Plan, a Lutz Plan, a Bernstein Plan, a Harrod Plan, and others. Mainline American economists became apologists for persistent American payments deficits, arguing that expanding world trade required enormous liquidity that could be satisfied only with dollars.

To many economists, central bankers, and treasury officials it is obvious that the persistent American payments deficits and consequent loss of gold reserves in the 1960s and 1970s are simply the "mirror image" of those West European and Japanese payments surpluses and growing national reserves during the 1960s and 1970s. As a result West Europeans and Japanese had been permitted to divert their own tax revenues to domestic improvements and social services while observers had begun to comment on the shabbiness of American cities. Between 1946 and 1958 the United States gave military grants of $16.6 billion to Western Europe and $6.1 billion to other countries; the first eight years of the Marshall Plan cost the American taxpayers $53 billion: The period of lend-lease assistance from July 1, 1940, to July 1, 1945, cost the American taxpayers a net of recouped assistance and payments of about $41 billion. America's West European and Japanese partners insisted on every advantage they had gained since 1945—long after the justifications for American generosity had vanished. On the other hand, Ludwig Erhard of West Germany in his *The Economics of Success* argues that American negotiations have remained remarkably soft-hearted, and soft-headed, regarding American expenditures for the defense of Western Europe.[10]

Matters are not helped by such ventures as President Johnson's Great Society and federal spending programs that undoubtedly appealed to many American voters. Federal budget deficits began to get out of hand. Foreign bankers began to lose confidence in American ability to manage the Bretton Woods system. Clearly, a retrenchment was in order to end the chronic disequilibrium in American payments accounts. As countless currencies depreciated against the dollar in the 1960s, American industry suffered unnecessary unemployment while capital, technology, and jobs moved abroad, primarily to Western Europe and Japan. To be sure, American consumers benefited from cheaper imports and relatively in- expensive foreign travel.

The American dollar did reap "benefits" as well as "costs" in serving the functions of an international currency. Such a role enables the United States to acquire and run a larger cumulative deficit than otherwise, since foreigners are willing to acquire and hold dollars. By creating "international money" in the form of dollars, Americans obtain claims of foreign resources much the same way as the gain from seignorage of an earlier period, when the state treasury gained the difference between the circulating value of a coin and the cost of bullion and its minting. With a "cumulative" deficit in its balance of payments, the United States can create internationally held dollars in a costless fashion and gain an increase in real national expenditure relative to national income. These arrangements also facilitated mobilization of resources to carry out American worldwide commitments made necessary by the cold war confrontation.

The cost side is that the United States gives up a substantial degree of freedom in conducting expansionary monetary and fiscal policies for strictly domestic purposes. Evidently by 1971 President Nixon felt that costs exceeded benefits derived from the dollar's role as an international currency. Coincidently, efforts toward détente began to make serious headway during the Nixon administration and the dollar's slippage as a world currency.

The Smithsonian Agreement of December 1971, a sort of crisis control rather than a reform as such, lasted little more than a year when massive currency flows led to national currency controls and proliferation of currency rates. By March 1973 all major world currencies were floating. Management was left to the market and to central bankers who intervened to prevent extreme fluctuations.

By 1972 a Committee on Reform of the International Monetary System and Related Issues, the Committee of Twenty, had been established within the IMF to develop a major reform of the international monetary system. The Committee of Twenty consisted of ten industrial countries and ten developing countries. The charge to the committee was to come up with new means of managing the quantity of international reserves, developing new adjustment mechanisms, and establishing a generally accepted currency or currencies.

There was general agreement of principles within the Committee of Twenty, which reported that exchange rates were to be more flexible (including floating rates in some circumstances); inconvertible balances, especially dollar balances, were to be returned to convertibility; the adjustment process was to be made more equitable; and cooperation was necessary to stem disequilibriating capital flows.

Principles are one thing; practice is another. Very serious differences soon came to surface. There was little compromise. Disagreements arose over the nature of controls on surplus and deficit countries, over conditions of floating, over the role of the dollar and gold, over conditions for dollar convertibility, and each country pushed its own views to the limit.

While the Committee of Twenty debated, the international monetary system received shocks that demolished existing systems of fixed exchange rates. Inflation fed by the large dollar outflow from the United States escalated to double digits in many countries. The issue was no longer inadequate international liquidity with which the committee was wrestling but one of excess liquidity. Different rates of national inflation undermined solutions to stable exchange rates. Indeed the emphasis was now on floating rates so as to shore up the domestic economy from international inflation.

The second shock came from OPEC countries, which engineered a significant rise in oil prices. The net effect was to transfer an estimated $70 billion from oil-consuming to oil-exporting countries in 1974. This brought major new problems of recycling the surplus earnings of oil producers, which in 1974 amounted to $150 billion. Indications at that time suggested that such surplus earnings would continue to constitute a problem. The recycling problem for the international monetary system, simply stated, was how to transfer earnings from oil-surplus to oil-deficit countries.

The recycling has been accomplished, for the most part, through private banks that accepted deposits of oil-surplus countries and loaned these funds to oil-importing countries, through government-to-government direct investment and loans, and the participation of the IMF and World Bank by borrowing from oil-producing and lending to oil-consuming countries. In any case, the sums in need of recycling were growing so rapidly that they in effect amounted to continual shocks to the system.

As a result, the committee capitulated, declaring that it was impossible to develop a comprehensive plan for monetary reform in view of the international economic situation. An interim committee was appointed to deal with more short-run problems such as oil-price increases and various recycling schemes.

By late 1975 and early 1976 agreement of sorts was reached on the mechanism for cooperation (January 1976, Jamaica Meeting) but not in the management of floating currencies. No agreement on the dollar was reached, nor on Special Drawing Rights (SDRs), nor indeed on gold as an international reserve asset. A movement was made toward demonetization of gold as an international reserve asset. This was encouraged by the elimination of an official price of gold at the IMF, proposed disposal of one-third of the Fund's supply of gold, and removal of IMF's obligation to make and receive payments in gold. The net effect is that the nature and quantity of what is to serve as an international reserve asset is outside the realm of international monetary management. With the reforms incomplete, the international monetary system continues to drift.

Little wonder that international monetary problems are as

fascinating as they are perplexing—combining as they do a rich mixture of technical economics, political repercussions, and even psychology of symbols and beliefs. The lessons from postwar experience suggest that embittered, politically bargained agreements on the international monetary system are untenable and surely give invitation to circumvent such agreements.

The United States and Great Britain proposed a postwar international monetary system organized to cope with many of the interwar problems. They reasoned that the determination of exchange rates, the provision of international liquidity, and the adjustment process are matters of political economy far too important to be left to the initiative of others. Accordingly, the Bretton Woods system dominated by British and American influence served to usher into being the International Monetary Fund. It was to serve as a source of short-term international liquidity, thereby providing countries time for balance-of-payments adjustments without resort to competitive currency devaluations and disarray of the interwar period.

By the 1970s, however, the Bretton Woods system was politically undermined and in a shambles, with its leadership weakened and its power challenged. Though the dominant political and economic power remained with the developed and industrialized countries led by the United States, such outsiders as Third World countries and the Soviet Union and its East European allies challenged the right of industrialized countries to manage the system. They, too, wanted to participate in the management and share what they observed as the rewards of the international economic system. The developed countries, for the most part, were just as determined to deny these outsiders access and share in the management.

At the close of the 1970s the world counted up its toll of unsolved problems. Inflation and unemployment were both simultaneous, the task of recycling funds from rich to poor was already immense, currencies were floating, and interest rates were high enough to set the course for another decade of inadequate investment.

Gold, which was supposed to be "demonitized" when the

United States stopped converting dollars into gold in August 1971 while the IMF in January 1976 agreed to start selling its gold stock and central bankers agreed to freeze their holdings, made a robust comeback. The European monetary system required 25 percent of its gold reserves in European currency units (ECUs). The United States was selling gold to help cover its trade deficit while other countries added to their gold reserves. In 1970 gold made up 41 percent of the world's official international reserves, while at the end of the decade demonetized gold accounted for 46 percent.

Floating exchanges had not been adopted by all countries. In fact, at the close of the 1970s, of the 142 members of the IMF, 41 were still pegged to the dollar, 14 to the French franc, and 3 to the British pound. The European monetary system embraced 8, and 38 were fixed on some other currency composite or set of indicators. Indeed, only 38 float freely in theory and still fewer in fact.

The major currencies all floated more or less dirtily against the dollar. *The Economist* noted several reasons for such behavior. In the first place it is argued that exchange rate movements do not correct trade imbalances. Their effects on inflation quickly erode the change in competitive advantages.[11] This is not strictly correct, as witness the swing from surplus to deficit by strong currencies in Japan and Germany in 1977–1979, or Great Britain's export boom in 1977, before the pound sterling rose too high.

Second, in the very short run, depreciation makes deficits worse, not better. While trade deficits are sliding down the front of the "J" curve, floating exchange markets may go on reacting, turning helpful adjustments into overadjustment. Third, exchange rate "uncertainty" makes trade and, still more, investment difficult according to many businessmen. One among many other complaints is that of complications about dealing in forward markets for currency. Fourth, the "weak" dollar, according to some, necessitated heavy intervention into the market.

The SDRs, which promised to displace the dollar and so protected the international monetary system from the vagaries of the American economy, did not live up to expectations.

Indeed, some $13.5 billion in SDRs had been allocated by the end of the decade. They were made a little more attractive by a more generous interest rate formula. In fact, governments were discussing ways in which the world's overload of dollar reserves might be sterilized in a substitution account, supplying holders with SDR-dominated assets in exchange. Nevertheless, the dollar closed the decade as the principal component in the international monetary system.

It is in the Third World, however, that even more serious troubles appeared. Blasted by chill winds blowing from the Organization of Petroleum Exporting Countries (OPEC), which compounded their deficit problems, they turned for relief to the industrial countries. Thanks to these countries and their successful reaction to the OPEC price shocks, the world avoided the dire predictions by commercial banks and the international business community of financial collapse and default. Nevertheless, by the end of the decade many of these countries were struggling under the weight of severe debt problems, which will be discussed briefly.

The problem of recycling petrodollars was eased by assistance from the industrial countries which rose from a net $6.8 billion in its peak year of 1977. Part went through special funds raised and loaned by the IMF. International banking boomed as a result of recycling. By the end of the 1970s "offshore" lending through such Euromarket centers as London and the Caribbean amounted to $60 billion.

Indeed, the Euromarkets had expanded to a gross $1,000 billion by the end of the decade. Most major banks had established an international network of branches, subsidiaries, and affiliates. In fact, one-third of their loans and profits were abroad.

To help stave off future crises, the IMF in early 1980 came forth with a "new" idea for a reserve asset backed by gold. Thanks to American actions freezing Iranian assets in November 1979, international financial officials pushed for the creation of a new reserve asset that could not be blocked or depreciated by any single government. With the dollar surpluses of oil-rich countries amounting to about $100 billion in 1980, world concern increased that so many dollars loose in world money markets could wreck the entire international monetary and financial organization.

In addition to reluctance on the part of some developed countries for a gold-backed substitution account, Third World countries are also opposed to using gold for any new scheme. Sales of IMF gold generate resources to assist the development of these countries and any attempt to use gold for another purpose is viewed by the Third World as depriving them of such resources.

FLEXIBLE (OR FLOATING) EXCHANGE RATES?

Therefore, the collapse of the Bretton Woods agreement was brought about by a combination of circumstances. Accelerating inflation in the United States acquired economic strength by Europe and Japan, coupled with large capital flows and an exchange rate that had not been changed since World War II. The system's end came in 1971, as we noted, when President Nixon, convinced that a run on the dollar was reaching alarming proportions, ordered the closing of the gold window. After months of last-ditch efforts to set new fixed exchange rates, the world officially turned to floating rates in March 1973. For some countries attempts to maintain a fixed parity turned out to be very expensive. Germany's central bank, for instance, lost $10 billion in 1983 prices in a fruitless attempt to maintain parity between the mark and the dollar.

It was expected that a system of floating exchange rates would put to rest problems that plagued the fixed exchange rate system of Bretton Woods. Henceforth markets would set exchange rates; the system would be self-correcting.

In practice, however, it turned out that the world was not in a freely floating or freely flexible exchange rate system as envisioned by theory. Some of the constraints were removed that had served as benchmarks and put pressure on governments to adjust their economic policies when exchange rates were out of line. By maintaining a low-valued yen, Japan, for instance, increased the competitiveness of its goods and services while protecting itself from high unemployment. In effect, the freedom to ignore the pre–1971 rules has become the freedom to devalue, to inflate, and to exclude foreign competition from home markets.

Given the turbulent years of the 1970s, however, the floating rate system has performed reasonably well. There is very little evidence that the system of floating exchange rates has caused more inflation or reduced the volume of trade. Rather than abandon the system, some critics would opt for more intervention by government in foreign exchange markets. Such intervention would presumably send a signal by the authorities to the speculators when the latter have pushed the currency too far.

Intervention appears to be a useless exercise. The markets usually win these games at considerable cost to intervening central banks and monetary authorities. Once inflation, for instance, is brought down and under control the existing system will become less volatile. Intervention, moreover, can be seen as a substitute for policy. Dollar creation, whether by the Federal Reserve or foreign desk, is still dollar creation.

The Reagan administration during the first half of the 1980s resisted pressure from abroad to create dollars as a way of making other currencies look stronger in the exchange markets. To a degree this policy had its source in monetarist views prevalent in the Reagan administration that dictate that a currency float should be a real float with no market-distorting interventions. There is a more practical reason as well. If you do not intervene, other motives that want to keep currencies on a par have only one option available—pursuit of sound economic policies. In short, the United States can unilaterally apply discipline to the world economy and save the world a lot of inflationary grief, restoring something approximating the old Bretton Woods system that was based on a strong gold-linked dollar.

Politicians, of course, resist monetary discipline, which is why Bretton Woods broke down. Politicians, both in the United States and abroad, have their own political agenda. Intervention in the foreign exchange markets, for instance, may show U.S. goodwill, but no amount of it will change economic fundamentals. Indeed, this appears to have been the case in the 1985 attempts to bring the dollar down.

Compromise proposals advanced by some economists (for example, Ronald McKinnon) would establish *target zones* for the dollar, yen, and mark. The United States, Japan, and Germany then would pledge to keep their currency values within those values. This would require considerable coordination among the three countries. Their monetary and fiscal policies would have to be aimed at maintaining the agreed-upon exchange rates. They would also be obliged, when necessary, to intervene in the exchange markets to maintain their rates.

Critics argue that such an arrangement has too many of the disadvantages of floating exchange rates and too many of the burdens of the fixed exchange rate system. In fact, the governments would also be required to set target zones for inflation and for real interest rates as well. If they could accomplish all of this there would be no need for an exchange-rate target since the exchange rates themselves would be stable.

It is unclear how far the negotiations among major industrial countries will go toward overhauling the present system. France and Italy push for a return to fixed-rate system. The U.S. program on the other hand calls for preserving the existing system and a wait-and-see attitude. Britain and Germany tend to agree with the U.S. view.

Despite Washington's reluctance, some observers believe that a new international monetary conference is inevitable, even though it may be a few years away. If so the theory of cooperation, which I discuss elsewhere as an approach to resolving the world debt issue, should serve as a guide to the participants: Do not be envious, do not be the first to defect, reciprocate both defection and cooperation, and do not be too clever.[12]

NOTES

1. See, for instance, George Macesich, *The International Monetary Economy and The Third World* (New York: Praeger, 1981), p. 52.

2. See Keynes's speech before House of Lords, May 23, 1944, reprinted in G. M. Meier, *Problems of World Monetary Order* (Oxford: Oxford University Press, 1974), p. 35.

3. F. A. Hayek, "A Commodity Reserve Currency," *Economic Journal*, June-September, 1943.

4. George Macesich, *The Politics of Monetarism: Its Historical and Institutional Development*, (Totowa, N.J.: Rowman and Allanheld, 1984).

5. J. M. Keynes, "The Objective of International Monetary Stability," *Economic Journal*, June-September 1943, pp. 185–87.

6. Keynes, *Ibid.*

7. Keynes, *Ibid.*

8. F. A. Hayek, *A Tiger by the Tail: The Keynesian Legacy of Inflation* (San Francisco: Cato Institute, 1979), pp. 107–8.

9. Robert Triffin, *The Evolution of the International Monetary System: Reappraisal and Further Perspectives* (Princeton, N.J.: Princeton Studies in International Finance, No. 12, 1964).

10. Ludwig Erhard, *The Economics of Success* (Princeton, N.J.: Van Nostrand, 1963).

11. *The Economist*, December 8, 1979.

12. George Macesich, *World Banking and Finance* (New York, N.Y.: Praeger, 1984).

CHAPTER 3

Are We All Monetarists Now?

WHAT IS MONETARISM?

A few years ago Sir Keith Joseph claimed: "We are all monetarists now."[1] What does this mean in terms of policy? Milton Friedman writes that a monetarist policy has five points:

first, the target should be growth in some monetary aggregate—just which aggregate is a separate question; second, monetary authorities should adopt long-run targets for monetary growth that are consistent with no inflation; third, present rates of growth of monetary aggregates should be modified to achieve the long-run targets in a gradual, systematic and preannounced fashion; fourth, monetary authorities should avoid fine-tuning; fifth, monetary authorities should avoid trying to manipulate either interest rates or exchange rates.[2]

He goes on to say that

almost any central banker in the world today agrees verbally to at least the first three of these five points, and most also to the fourth. The fifth is unquestionably the most controversial. However, in most cases the profession of faith is simply lip service.[3]

Thus, in major industrial countries monetary targets have become the preferred economic lever. Revelation? A truce between Keynesians and monetarists? Fashion? Or desperation? All four, argues *The Economist*.[4]

Rapid growth in the money supplies in nearly all countries was followed by inflation in the 1970s. Monetary targetry was the instrument used by countries that appeared the most stable. Such a strategy came to be equated with all that was stable, noninterfering, and free market. Strong countries that believed in money targets were increasingly having to come to the rescue of the very weak, who were constrained to pay attention to their rescuer's beliefs. In many countries there was disenchantment with past and current fiscal policy as an instrument for stabilizing the economy. Fine-tuning also had passed into disrepute. In short, experience in many countries suggests that monetary policy is not an effective instrument for achieving full employment or economic growth. It is best in promoting price stability over the long run.

At the very least, monetarism serves as an early-warning system to governments. Monetary targets, as such, are not very meaningful when they are nice and easy to hit, nor when they are rolled over. They then become little more than a forecasting exercise, as central banks simply adjust their sights after each regrettable monetary lapse. Monetary targets must signify a government's intention not to expand the money supply to accommodate wage and price pressures originating in various sectors of the economy. In effect, the focus of monetary policy must be on control of the absolute level of prices. Again, it is an issue of credibility. On this score there is a significant difference between rhetoric and practice of monetarist policies.

Friedman's observation regarding the last of his five points as the most controversial of monetarist policy may well serve to undermine the other four. As noted above, there is a movement in Europe and elsewhere to pressure the U.S. administration to intervene in foreign exchange markets to reduce fluctuations in currency values. In effect, Europeans hope that Americans will share with them the burden of currency intervention. Similarly, it is hoped that the American administration will "do something" about high interest rates.

The ultimate objective is to undermine the course of American monetary policy perceived by some people as "too mone-tarist." This contention is disputed by most monetarists who argue that American monetary policy is simply not monetar-ist.

Attempts to keep the dollar down have had undesirable do-mestic effects in those countries attempting to do so. The do-mestic impact of intervention has been to reduce the money supply in interventionist's co-countries, such as Germany, Belgium, and the Netherlands. The cost to Europeans and others of such intervention has been to intensify recession in their countries. Attempts to substitute an official view of cur-rency values for that of a free market are seldom successful and often costly—the moderate success of depressing the dol-lar in 1985 notwithstanding.

Nevertheless, the Europeans, as we noted, are adamant in pushing the case for intervention. The French, for example, are proposing a "tripolar" monetary system based on the dol-lar, the yen, and the European Monetary System. Under the new system, an exchange rate zone would be established for the currency blocs, and central banks would be obligated to keep rate movements within these zones. As such, the idea represents a partial return to the Bretton Woods system of fixed exchange rates and would require ongoing intervention in foreign exchange markets. If the movements of a currency were too great for intervention to handle, a country would have to alter its domestic economic policies.

Under the French plan, central banks would, presumably, have to stabilize interest rates and exchange rates rather than concentrating primarily on controlling monetary aggregates. For reasons already discussed, this is a sure road to rekin-dling inflation. It is not surprising that the French plan has been received with something less than enthusiasm. The Americans, British, and Germans seem to agree that the eco-nomic fundamentals of inflation rates and trade balances are the primary determinants of exchange rates, and that move-ments caused by these fundamentals cannot be countered for long by intervention.

Indeed, at the Bonn economic summit in May 1985 calls were heard once again urging that the summit launch an international monetary conference to establish formal links between the U.S. dollar, the Japanese yen, and the European currency unit in order to "stabilize" exchange rates and promote world trade and economic growth. However, a leading monetarist politician, Mrs. Margaret Thatcher, said: "When people don't know what to do they propose to have a conference about it. It's not really very constructive. It's an admission of failure." Moreover, the British prime minister went on to add that calls for government agreements to stabilize exchange rates lacked precision and she termed some "generalized jabberwocky."[5]

At the same time, she ruled out attempts at inflation to promote growth in Europe and Britain because "normally that means printing money and that only sows the seeds of future trouble." Adding to the money supply, in her view, leads to inflation and "is a fraud on the savings of everyone . . . it really isn't a good policy for any government. I always try to remind people that it was inflation that cracked and broke the Bretton Woods fixed exchnge system."[6]

Developing or Third World countries are even more reluctant to introduce flexible exchange rates. More than 40 percent of these countries (in 1985) still peg their currencies to one or another of the leading currencies.[7] Since their inflation rates are typically greater than those of the leading industrial countries, the fixed exchange rates of the developing countries soon become overvalued.

This drives some developing countries to adopt multiple exchange rates—one for trade, one for financial transactions, and so on. Other Third World countries adopt more direct controls. The net result, typically, is to make the country's domestic industry even more uncompetitive in the world market. Another consequence of an overvalued exchange rate is to make all things foreign seem cheaper, including foreign loans, so countries have a beguiling way of financing their deficits.

Interest rates are the other candidates most likely to provoke disagreement and controversy over monetarist policy. Some evidence suggests that higher and more variable money growth since 1967 in the United States has been primarily responsible for the longer-term rise and increased variability in interest rates.[8] The longer-term evidence does not appear to support such special factors as a significant change in the behavior of velocity or real output growth. This suggests that an extended period of lower and less variable money growth may very well generate lower and more stable interest rates, which is what monetarists advocate.

PRESENT STATUS

How are we to get from here to there? Monetarist ·policy calls for present monetary aggregate growth rates to be reduced gradually to achieve long-run targets consistent with no inflation in a systematic and preannounced fashion. The emphasis on the "gradual, systematic, and preannounced" manner underscored by Friedman will help keep transitional costs politically acceptable. Such evidence as we have on the costs and benefits of inflation control does appear consistent with a gradualist approach.

It is in the control of inflation that the credibility of the monetary authority becomes absolutely essential. If the purpose of the monetary targets is their declaratory effect, flexibility—that is, rolling targets—will have the same effect as flexibility in other targets. All bend together, undermining the credibility of the monetary authority.

Monetary rules are urged by monetarists to provide the monetary authority with guidelines that will enhance its credibility. I have discussed elsewhere the issue of credibility, which is indeed a fundamental one.[9] Unfortunately, even if these rules are adopted, it is likely that the long duration of bureaucratic inertia and behavior in terms of self-interest will simply emasculate the rules. Indeed, Friedman writes:

Why the enormous resistance of the Fed to moving to monetary aggregates? Fundamentally, I believe, because monetary aggregates permit for more effective monitoring of performance and accountability for achieving targets than money market conditions. . . . Who of us wants to be held responsible for our mistakes? It's not very nice to have a bottom line, why should we introduce one?[10]

There are alternatives to a strict bottom line for the Federal Reserve System. We have discussed elsewhere institutional arrangements under which central banks in other countries operate.[11] Friedman proposes either to make the Fed a bureau in the Treasury under the Secretary of Treasury, or to put it under direct congressional control. "Either involves terminating the so-called independence of the system. But either would establish a strong incentive for the Fed to produce a stabler monetary environment than we have had."[12]

Federal Reserve representatives repeatedly argue that there is little the Fed can do to control monetary growth along monetarist lines "under current operating procedures." Monetarists argue that these "procedures" are nothing more than self-imposed restrictions. They are, in fact, what monetarists want changed in order to improve effectiveness and credibility of the Federal Reserve. Allan Meltzer argues:

> We want to change those rules. Their own research by Kien and others we have mentioned and by virtually every academic economist who has studied this supports our view. Our ideas have found their way into the market place, into the press, to governments here and in foreign countries. The Swiss are able to control money growth rates with high variability, but with strong belief that when they announce a target, it is going to be achieved. Their experience could be duplicated here. It is not the variability, it is the credibility of the policy that is important.[13]

Monetarism incorporates principles that are widely accepted and to which, unfortunately, some central banks pay only lip service. It may well be, as some of its detractors would have it, that the whole world groaned and marveled to find itself monetarist. Monetarism's adoption and apparent triumph are not necessarily the beginnings of its downfall. It is not that the theory was correct until it was freely put into practice. If put into full practice, monetarism will survive the experience.

WHICH "MONETARISM" TO ADOPT?

Which monetarism shall countries put into practice? Shall it be the older version of monetarism as advocated by Milton

Friedman and people of similar views, or the "newer" version as pushed by the "new classical macroeconomists," or the "pragmatic monetarism" of most central bankers, or, indeed, is there a difference? This study argues that there are important theoretical empirical and policy differences among the several views. The architects of policy would do well to read all but push from theory to policy the older version of monetarism. The analysis and evidence drawn from several countries and presented and discussed in this study suggest that the newer versions of monetarism, if indeed they are monetarist, may not be as useful at this stage of history as the older version for purposes of policy.

As it is in most revolutions and counterrevolutions, the Keynesian revolu⁚on and postrevolutionary era has taken on several meanings, so it is that monetarism and its counterrevolutions have taken a similar course. Friedman thus identifies monetarism with the quantity theory of money, suggesting thereby that monetarism is not a new development. It is also consistent with the quantity theory he freed of dependence on the assumption of automatic full employment, the focal point of the Keynesian ridicule of traditional quantity theory. In Friedman's University of Chicago monetary workshop during the 1950s (in which this writer had the privilege of participating as a graduate student), studies on inflation and the role of money in inflation received considerable attention. Friedman's work changed professional thinking on matters pertaining to the role of money.

The monetarist view, as summarized by Friedman in *Counter-Revolution in Monetary Theory*, questions the doctrine pushed by John Maynard Keynes that variation in government spending, taxes, and the national debt could stabilize both the price level and the real economy.[14] This doctrine has come to be called "the Keynesian Revolution."

Friedman monetarists never completely shut the door on countercyclical policies and demand management. To be sure, they advise against such manipulation of stabilization policies. If pressed, however, some of them would resort to stimulative measures of the economy when unemployment, for instance, was unnaturally high and when such measures could speed up the economy's return to the natural rate of unemployment without adding to inflation.

The newer vintage monetarists and other apostles of the "new classical macroeconomics" have no reservation about casting out and repudiating such measures on the part of government. Drawing on support from "rational expectation theory" they argue that monetary policies can never alter unemployment except temporarily when the central bank moves to surprise and fool the public. This is only a temporary situation. Once the new policy is generally understood and expected it will have no real effects at all on the real variables in an economy; it will be absorbed in prices.

Thus, in its extreme form, the newer version of "monetarism" asserts that people will always offset any known systematic government policy to generate employment and output. This assertion is questioned by the older version of monetarism. The central monetarist result remains. The long-term effect of an increase in the rate of growth of the money supply is an increase in the rate of inflation.

To the architects of monetary policy, monetarists of earlier persuasion put forward three main objectives of such policy: (1) maintain liquidity in the very short run; (2) avoid inducing fluctuations in the short to medium run; and (3) control inflation in the long run.

The policy of steady long-term growth in the money supply is the circumstance of the Friedman-type monetarism. It hinges first on the predictability and stability of short-run, transitory shifts in money demand. To be sure, some of the older-vintage monetarists feel that it is possible to recognize and offset the short-run changes in the demand for money without risk to their ultimate aim of controlling inflation. If they cannot "fine tune" policy, they are confident of making the necessary adjustments without risking inflation. The evidence thus far certainly does not strongly support confidence in fine-tuning policies.

The international dimensions of monetarist policy determine the type of exchange rate system feasible. Truly fixed exchange rates with free international capital movements would make the control of monetary aggregates impossible. An increase in the money supply, for instance, would stimulate demand and prices, and increase net imports. In a system of free exchange rates, any variation in a country's money supply, relative to those of its trading partners, will be mirrored in movements of exchange rates. Thus it is that only a freely flexible exchange rate system would be compatible with a steady monetary growth.

Monetarist policies are possible in the current "managed" system of exchange rates, provided the exchange rates are allowed to move sufficiently to offset any substantial monetary leakages. The European Monetary System is illustrative of the point. Most industrial countries have reduced the trend rate of monetary growth. As monetarists promised, this has eventually moderated inflation. Most countries have also allowed erratic monetary growth, which has, in turn, produced oscillations in output and growth. This is also as monetarism predicts. Moreover, the high yields on long-term debt show that credit markets are anticipating new outbreaks of inflation. This suggests, as monetarists argue, that the issue of the credibility of monetary authorities remains unresolved.

NOTES

1. George Macesich, *Monetarism: Theory and Policy* (New York: Praeger Publishers, 1983), p. 228.
2. Milton Friedman, "Monetary Policy: Theory and Practice," *Journal of Money, Credit and Banking*, February 1982, p. 101.
3. *Ibid.*
4. *The Economist*, July 2, 1977, p. 20.
5. "Britain's Thatcher Dismisses French Plan to Fix Exchange Rates as 'Jabberwocky,'" *Wall Street Journal*, May 2, 1985, p. 34.
6. *Ibid.*
7. *The Economist*, May 18, 1985, p. 35.
8. See Macesich, *Monetarism: Theory and Policy*, p. 230.
9. *Ibid.*, p. 230.
10. Friedman, "Monetary Policy," p. 115. Friedman's paper contains a good historical documentation of the Federal Reserve System's attempt to steer clear of any course set for it by Congress.
11. See George Macesich, *The Politics of Monetarism: Its Historical and Institutional Development* (Totowa, N.J.: Rowman and Allanheld, 1984), p. 119.

12. Friedman, "Monetary Policy," p. 118.

13. A. Meltzer in "Is the Federal Reserve's Monetary Control Policy Misdirected?" *Journal of Money, Credit, and Banking*, February 1982, p. 146.

14. Milton Friedman, *The Counter-Revolution in Monetary Theory*, First Wincott Memorial Lecture (London: Institute of Economic Affairs, 1970).

CHAPTER 4

Monetarists, New Classicalism, and Rational Expectations

EMPIRICAL JUDGMENTS AND THEORETICAL SIMILARITIES

The empirical judgments of the older monetarists and the new classicals are, in general, similar. In particular, both prefer that monetary policy be conducted by rules instead of by discretionary authority. Their theoretical directions to these judgments are not, however, always identical.

There are, of course, important theoretical similarities. Both assert that only real magnitudes matter for real decisions and continuous optimization. This is satisfactory for a static framework. The issue is how to carry these features over to the dynamic problem. The rational expectation hypothesis serves such a requirement. The hypothesis implies that what agents do expect is, within a serially uncorrelated error, what the true model says they should expect. Thus, assurance is provided that agents will be successful and consistent.

To be sure, not everyone who uses the rational expectations hypothesis in their analyses is, strictly speaking, an adherent of "new classicalism."[1] The hypothesis is convenient for introducing endogenous expectations into an economic model. An analyst may use the rational expectation hypothesis and not adhere to the other two tenets of new classicalism—that only real phenomena matter and that agents are consistent and successful optimizers.

Much of the new classicalism, however, originates with the early work of such monetarists as Milton Friedman. Such ideas as holding the money supply responsible for inflation, unemployment as a response to real wages, and concomitant failure of the Phillips curve trade-off between unemployment and the rate of increase of wages are directly linked to Friedman's early studies. Indeed, the distinction between nominal and real quantities made by Friedman, and which enables him to construct a theory of inflation, is one of his fundamental contributions. It serves his argument that money is neutral in the long run but not necessarily in the short run.

MONEY'S EFFECT ON OUTPUT AND INTEREST RATES

Consider, for instance, Friedman's view of money's effect on output and interest rates. He accepts that the price level is passive. "Nominal money" refers to the money stock, or the actual dollar (dinar, pound, franc, and so on) amount of money in the economy. Real cash balances, on the other hand, can be thought of as the total dollar amount of money adjusted for changes in the price levels. If, for example, the nominal money stock stays constant but prices double, the amount of real cash balances in the system can be thought of as declining by 50 percent. The quantity theorist or monetarist of Friedman's persuasion assumes that the nominal quantity of money can be controlled by the monetary authorities, but that the amount of real cash balances is determined by activities within the economic system.

The relationship between changes in nominal money and changes in real cash balances lies at the heart of the quantity theory of money. Increasing (or decreasing) the rate of growth of the money supply is hypothesized to leave households and businesses with excess (or deficient) cash balances. People have three options with which to dispose of these excess funds: they can purchase credit instruments, they can purchase goods and services, or they can do both. Increasing the demand for goods and services will affect prices, however. This, in turn, will affect the level of real cash balances.

The extent of an increase in real cash balances depends on the extent to which prices change. Generally speaking, in periods of high employment—such as during a boom period—increases in the amount of nominal money would be expected to lead to an increase in prices.

The second major aspect of the quantity theory and monetarist position is the relationship between changes in the nominal quantity of money, in prices, and in interest rates. To explain this relationship, quantity theorists and monetarists like to talk about three effects of changes in the rate of growth in the money supply on interest rates: the liquidity effect, the income effect, and the price anticipation effect. The magnitude of each of these effects and the time lag before they are felt depend, in part, on how fully employed the economy's resources are.

The first to be felt is the liquidity effect. This results from the fact that increasing (or decreasing) the rate of growth of the money supply will leave households and businesses with more (or less) money than they wish to hold. Increases cause them to shift some portion of these excess balances into credit instruments, increasing the price of these instruments, and, therefore, decreasing interest rates. According to the quantity theorists and monetarists, increasing the stock of money will also lead to an increase in the demand for goods and services. This will stimulate, after a three- to six-month lag, the demand for credit on the part of businesses and households. This increased demand for credit, called the income effect, leads to a decline in the price of credit instruments and an increase in market interest rates.

In addition, the quantity theorists and monetarists say, the increased aggregate demand for goods and services will increase prices. The amount of inflation, however, depends upon the extent to which resources are employed. More important, as households and businesses begin to feel the effect of inflation, they expect more of it. This, in turn, will add to the credit demand. If people expect prices to increase and if interest rates are low, it is logical that people will want to go into debt.

The increase in demand for credit caused by inflationary price expectations leads to the price anticipation effect on interest rates. Lenders also come to expect inflation and therefore require a higher return to compensate for the expected loss in purchasing power.

As a result of this price anticipation effect, quantity theorists and monetarists like to speak of interest rates as being made up of two parts: One portion relates to the "real" (or natural) return on capital assets (assuming no expected inflation), while a second portion relates to changes in expected prices.

Let us assume an individual anticipates no inflation and receives a 4 percent return on investment. Now let events change and assume the individual anticipates 3 percent inflation to continue indefinitely. It is hard to be content with a 4 percent return. Instead, the individual will want the 4 percent return plus 3 percent additional to compensate for the expected inflation. Market interest rates thus reflect these price expectations.

This theory explains the often heard contention by quantity theorists and monetarists that increasing the money supply, while admittedly decreasing interest rates in the short run (the liquidity effect), will eventually lead to higher interest rates (the income and price effects). Because quantity theorists and monetarists believe the economy is inherently stable, they contend that the real rate of interest, as opposed to the market rate of interest, does not change very much. Therefore, most of the changes that are observed in the market rate of interest result from erratic historical changes in the money supply.

The new classical view does not dispute these issues; they are in fact incorporated in the new classical models. In their view money is not only neutral in the long run but in the short run as well. This is, of course, an important difference beween Friedman-type monetarists and the new classical economists.

At the same time the two views are similar in that both underscore the importance of a natural rate of unemployment as well as a natural rate of interest and a natural rate of output. All three are, presumably, the results produced by the equations in a Walrasian system of general equilibrium with appropriate structural characteristics of the various markets included. This similarity has led some economists to classify both views as "monetarist."[2]

PHILLIPS CURVE

The issues at hand are readily illustrated in the expectations-augmented Phillips curve. Mathematically, the expectations-augmented Phillip's curve can be stated as

$$W = f(U) + \beta P^e \tag{1}$$

where W = rate of wage change
      U = unemployment
      P^e = expected rate of inflation[3]

Friedman monetarists argue that in the long run $\beta = 1$ so that the expected rate of wage increase is equal to a component of excess demand plus the expected rate of inflation. The Phillips curve is vertical. The rate of increase in money wages is equal to the expected rate of inflation.

There is thus no long-run trade-off between unemployment and inflation. A short-run trade-off may be had, but only at the expense of faster inflation by the monetarists. This assumes, of course, that inflation is fully anticipated. If it is not, the coefficient β in Equation 1 would be less than one. In this case the slope of the long-run Phillips curve is less than vertical but steeper than in the short run. There is, thus, some permanent trade-off between unemployment and inflation in the long run, but less so than in the short run. If $\beta = 0$, the short run and long run would be the same.

To judge from recent studies, the empirical evidence offers support to the monetarist view that $\beta = 1$. There appears to be no trade-off between unemployment and inflation in the long run. Not everyone however is convinced by the evidence. Indeed, Robert Solow (1969) produces results of $\beta = 0.4$ for the United Kingdom; S. J. Turnovsky (1972) presents results for Canada for β not significantly different from 1; R. B. Cross and David Laidler (1975) report on results for 20 countries and find no evidence of a long-run trade-off for any country.[4]

Milton Friedman and Edmund Phelps have independently questioned the theoretical validity of the Phillips curve as well as its applicability to policy matters.[5] In 1968 they argued that rational workers, unions, and firms will take account of inflation and expected inflation in setting wages and prices, so that deviations from the expected trend will be related to unemployment rates. The net effect is that the eventual inflation effects of a reduction in unemployment would be much greater than the initial impact. Subsequent events supported their analysis when after 1966 and into the 1970s inflation picked up speed while unemployment remained low.

Friedman and Phelps argue that there is really only one unemployment rate and it is what Friedman calls the natural rate at which wages and prices will continue on their antici- pated path irrespective of the implied inflation rate. Thus at- tempts to push down the unemployment rate below its natu- ral rate will result only in increasing inflation. Presumably if the unemployment rate is held above the natural rate infla- tion will decelerate and ultimately there will be an even faster deflation.

Problems of the Phillips curve aside, the short-run Phillips curve is at times used by some economists, in combination with the natural rate, to gauge the difficulty in reducing the prevailing inertial inflation by running the economy for a time at a higher than natural rate of unemployment. Where price expectations are brought down as a result, the economy can return to the natural rate without setting off inflation.

Do policy makers really know the natural rate? Can they gauge such a rate for policy purposes in a meaningful way? Briefly, they cannot.[6] Indeed the new classicals argue they should not even try. They extend the Friedman-Phelps argu- ment and consider the economy (including labor markets) as always in equilibrium with neither excess demand nor excess supply. Prices and wages exist to clear the markets given to the expectations that economic agents form with the information they have. The economy is thus, more or less, always at its natural rate, but this rate itself varies.

Policies themselves are, moreover, important inputs in the formation of economic expectations. As a result the behavior of policy makers in the formation and execution of policies is critical to the stability of the economy. Predictable behavior of the monetary authorities in the formation and execution of monetary policy is realized when such policy is conducted within a rules-oriented policy system in which the monetary authorities are constrained to carry out a prescribed rate of growth in the money supply. The net effect will be to allow the economy to settle to its correct-information natural rate of unemployment. Whatever the rate to which the economy moves and settles will be its natural rate.

Friedman monetarists also distinguish, as discussed above, between nominal and real or natural interest rates that are determined by a multiplicity of factors traditionally summarized in productivity and thrift. The importance of price expectations is emphasized, as in the expectations-augmented Phillip's curve.

Mathematically, the relationship can be expressed as

$$r = i + p^e \tag{2}$$

where r = market or nominal rate of interest
      i = real or natural rate of interest
     p^e = expected rate of inflation

In equilibrium, the real (or natural) rate of interest is determined by real factors largely independent of monetary changes. During transitional periods, which can be quite long, changes in the money supply cause real rates of interest to change owing to slow adjustment of actual and expected rates of inflation to monetary changes. Recent studies support the belief that inflation expectations play an important role in the determination of interest rates.

The importance of expectations was in fact underscored by Irving Fisher more than half a century ago.[7] Thus Fisher's specification of the formulation of expectations made the expected rate of inflation a distributed lag formation of past rates of inflation with the most recent observation most heavily weighted. Fisher's expectations model leads to the conclusion that individuals will underestimate the current rate of inflation if inflation is accelerating. He also recognized the implications of this forecasting bias for the trade-off between inflation and unemployment as early as 1926.

Friedman also recognizes as did Fisher that expectations of inflation are slow to develop.[8] Though the process has accelerated since the 1960s it still takes years—not days, weeks, or months—for expectations of inflation to fully respond to actual changes. This almost assures, for instance, some short-term trade-off between unemployment and inflation.

This is a conclusion that is not accepted by the new classicals. As with the neutrality of money they deny that such a short-term trade-off exists. In their view agents are continuously in equilibrium given their information. The new classicals' acceptance of the rational expectations hypothesis assures that except for random shocks the information available to the agents is correct. Thus an inverse relation between unemployment and inflation that is observed cannot be utilized even in the short run since it inflicts an unsystematic or random component of the relation between changes in individual workers' wage levels and/or producers' prices and the general rate of inflation.[9]

Related to Friedman's view that inflation expectations are slow to develop is his preference for rules versus discretionary authority. His particular rule for monetary policy is that money should be allowed to grow at a constant percent per year where the percent rate is determined by the secular rate of gross national product (GNP) growth allowing for secular changes in the velocity of money.

RULES VERSUS DISCRETIONARY AUTHORITY

The new classicals accept the Friedman monetarist position that rules are preferable to discretionary authority. Simply put, the monetarist message is that the monetary policy game without rules is self-destructive.[10] Monetarists or quantity theorists urge a policy system based on rules and nondiscretionary intervention into the economy. The principal policy corollary of the Friedman monetarists is that only a slow and steady rate of increase in the money supply—one in line with the real growth of the economy—can insure price stability.

In effect, the central issue in the on-going disagreement is over defined versus undefined or discretionary policy systems. On this score the new classicals and Friedman monetarists are on one side of the issue while modern Keynesians and central bankers whose position is that defined policy systems are inferior to administrative discretion are on the other side of the issue. The modern Keynesian position and that of central bankers does not involve a search for optimal decision rules for monetary (and fiscal) policy. Their preference is to place "the political economist at the President's elbow." Central bankers are more or less in accord since it is consistent with their view that the conduct of monetary policy is an "art" not to be encumbered by explicit policy rules.[11]

Monetarists and new classicals in their insistence on lawful policy systems and limitations on the undefined exercise of power by government are thus in direct conflict with modern Keynesians whose approach is, in effect, the economic branch of the political interventionist position whose defining principle is the extensive use of government power without definite guides or policy systems.[12] This approach has important allies in central banks with whom it shares many banking school ideas. Along with central bankers they strongly oppose the measurement of monetary policy by the money supply, whatever its definition. They apparently prefer to use interest rates and other credit market conditions as measures of monetary policy. Such a view is, in effect, similar to the now defunct views of the banking school that takes "sound credit conditions" as its guiding principle, rather than the money supply. Although many variants of the theory are possible, they typically take as a principal autonomous and explanatory variable some measure of credit conditions, amount of credit or bank credit, credit availability, credit terms, or interest rates. These measures are as important to central bankers today as they were almost two hundred years ago.

No doubt modern Keynesians do not consider themselves

heirs to the banking school tradition. Their strong rejection of the concept of the money supply, however, is similar to the banking school view. It is curiously intense and implacable.[13]

Impressive as the case for discretionary authority may be, we have it from the theory of bureaucracy that we can expect central bankers not to take seriously theory and empirical evidence that will constrain their activities.[14] This has little to do with central bankers, many of whom are outstanding. At issue is the system itself and the incentives to which central bankers respond.

Central banks as government agencies exercise discretionary policy. It is thus important to have an independent evaluation of their performance in terms of explicit criteria. Central banks are loath to accept this constraint since they view the exercise of monetary policy as an "art" that cannot be defined or measured in terms of a single variable. Their preference is to discuss monetary policy in terms of unmeasured variables such as the intention of policy makers or the state of monetary restraint, or else in terms of a set of nonequivalent measuring variables among which the interpreter is free to choose as he wishes.

A case in point illustrating well the issues involved is the experience cited by Milton Friedman in his exchange with Federal Reserve authorities. In describing a 1969 Federal Reserve conference on controlling monetary aggregate, he writes:

Prior and subsequent to this time, outside persons were invited to meet with members of the board in Washington from time to time. I attended many such meetings of so-called academic consultants. They were interesting experiences, no doubt instructive to the many Federal Reserve personnel who sat around the sides of the boardroom where the meeting was invariably held, without participating. However, I finally concluded that the meetings were called purely for window-dressing purposes. I was unable to detect any influence whatsoever exerted by the consultant's comments on the system's actions. Indeed, the choice of the particular consultants invited to attend seemed designed to guarantee offsetting and contradictory advice, leaving the Fed free to pursue its own devices. However, even on those rare occasions when something approaching a consensus emerged, I could detect no subsequent effect on policy.[15]

According to our theory of bureaucracy, this is what, in fact, we should expect. Policy making is an "art" that is heavily dependent on inside information and expertise. Consistent with the theory of bureaucracy, the Federal Reserve simply undercut and disregarded the knowledge that would constrain it. Thus in reply to a letter in 1969 from Friedman regarding Federal Reserve use of monetary aggregates as targets, Chairman William M. Martin writes:

I seriously doubt that we could ever attain complete control (of monetary aggregates), but I do think it quite true that we could come significantly closer to such control than we do now—if we wished to make that variable our exclusive target. But the wisdom of such an exclusive orientation of monetary policy is, of course, the basic question.[16]

Friedman's view of Martin's reply and what he later learned of the affair is certainly consistent with our theory.

That's a very instructive statement [Martin's]. First of all, it says what the Fed has repeatedly denied and was to deny throughout the rest of the period that I'm talking about, that it could control monetary aggregates. But second, the Fed didn't really mean it. The reply was simply designed to immobilize one—as I later learned from an economist in the Fed's Research Division, who boasted to me about his cleverness in constructing that reply. Of course, it did immobilize me. Why conduct a study to figure out how to do something the Fed already knew how to do?[17]

Again, as our theory suggests, it is the agency itself that is important and not individuals, distinguished though they may be. Thus in 1980, after Paul Volcker became chairman, Friedman wrote,

Monetary growth was put first and money market conditions second. However, that change turned out to be pure lip service and was later de-emphasized.

Congress passed Concurrent Resolution 133 in 1975, which expressed the sentiments of Congress that the Federal Reserve control monetary aggregates, and consult and report to Congress at regular intervals. This was a resolution strongly opposed by the Federal Reserve. When passed, the Federal Reserve undermined the resolution.[18]

If Congress has not been able to bend the Federal Reserve to its will, another study strongly suggests that since the Treasury-Federal Reserve accord of March 1951, American presidents have been, in fact, the principal political influence behind the Federal Reserve policy. According to the evidence cited in the study, Fed policy was significantly changed in 1953, 1961, 1969, 1971, 1974, and 1977—all years in which the presidency changed.[19] This is consistent with our theory, since risk avoidance would push the Fed to pay closer attention to presidential desires than to those of Congress. It is the president and his administration that can directly threaten the Fed's status as an agency.[20] The president does have the power to name the chairman of the Federal Reserve Board and at least two other members of the board during each presidential term. There is, moreover, a close working relationship between the administration and the Federal Reserve Board.

It is significant, for instance, that during the important monetary policy changes between 1950 and 1970, the same individual, William M. Martin, was chairman. The strong presidential influence under which the central bankers of the Federal Reserve operate is suggested by events during the tenure of President Johnson (1963–1969). These are also the years when market participants began to realize that significant changes were occurring in the country's monetary system away from a constrained specie-like system to an unconstrained government fiat standard.

Additional confirmation of presidential influence on the Fed is provided by the Nixon administration (1969–1974), when Arthur Burns served as chairman. In 1972, when Nixon was running for reelection, the money supply (the old M1 definition) grew at almost 6.5 percent during the last quarter of 1972 and the first quarter of 1973, or at better than 6 percent during the period 1969–1974. This is indeed, up to that period, a postwar record growth in the money supply. President Nixon also removed the country's last links with gold in 1971.

To this may be added the administration's futile attempts to hold down inflation by price and wage controls and guidelines while promoting an expansive monetary policy.

During the Ford and Carter years, monetary policy registered an indifferent performance. Ford succeeded in slowing monetary growth during his tenure (August 1974 to December 1976) by holding to his priority to bring down inflation. Arthur Burns was chairman of the Fed during this period.

Carter at first considered inflation a nonmonetary phenomenon and promoted monetary growth with the idea of lowering interest rates and encouraging investment. Arthur Burns continued to serve as Federal Reserve chairman until March 1978, when Carter appointed G. William Miller to the position. In November 1978 President Carter changed priorities from stimulating the economy to fighting inflation that spurted into double digits. From the previous high of over 8.5 percent rate of growth in the old M1 reached by October 1978, the money supply growth was slowed by March 1979. Thereafter it again took off with M1B growing at a 13 percent annual rate between March and October of 1979.

Paul Volcker became chairman of the Federal Reserve in August 1979. On October 6, 1979, he announced that the Federal Reserve would henceforth concentrate on directly controlling the money supply and deemphasize interest rates as targets. We have discussed elsewhere the performance of American monetary policy since 1979.[21] President Reagan's comments suggesting that it might be a good idea to put the Fed under Treasury supervision may well be a harbinger.

We should also expect that an agency such as the Federal Reserve in our example would push its own version of "history." Such activities can range from outright concealment of information that might be unfavorable to it or helpful to its critics, to pushing a general framework within which agency activities are interpreted so as to minimize the danger that it will be accused of making serious agency error.

On this score it is interesting that the Federal Reserve undertook an extensive examination of its experience with monetary aggregates. In a massive two-volume study, the conclusion reached is that "the basic operating procedure represents a sound approach to attaining long-run objectives set for monetary standards."[22]

Quite a few observers will agree with Friedman when he writes, "I believe that the fundamental explanation for the persistence and importance of bureaucratic inertia in the Federal Reserve System is the absence of a bottom line."[23] In short, the Federal Reserve System operates in a manner consistent with our theory of bureaucracy. It is such recognition that has prompted more fundamental proposals for monetary reform and which I discuss in another study.[24]

Since most central banks are concerned for their power and prestige, they will prefer policy systems of discretion. The more closely constrained their activities are by rules or performance criteria, the less their power and prestige. Understandably they have little desire to be demoted from the status of decision maker to that of a social errand boy. Their preference for such policy systems leads them to prefer economic models, or theories, that justify or support them. Since the class of policy system involves an undefined behavior of the instrumental variable, it is in general opposed to systematic theories, since these lead to defined optimal behavior of the instrumental variable (defined money-supply functions, for example), thus eliminating the rationale for central bank discretion. The central bank is led to prefer models in which the performance of the economic system is unknowable, indeterminate, and to deny existence of such knowledge that led to decision rules that would undermine its power. The central bank's risk avoidance impels it in the same direction. The more indefinite the state of knowledge, the less the likelihood that the central bank will ever successfully be demonstrated to have committed a serious error.[25]

Agreement with Friedman monetarists that rules are preferable to discretionary authority, however, does not mean that the new classicals completely accept Friedman's rule that the money supply should grow at a constant percent per year. The reason for their less than enthusiastic endorsement of Friedman's rule is that monetary policy cannot systematically trade off inflation for output or employment. Economic agents with rational expectations will understand the rule and thus not be fooled by changes in the money supply in moving away from the natural rate of unemployment or output. It is the determinateness and simplicity of the Friedman rule that the new classicals embrace. Since economic agents act as if they know the structure of the economy and since they must infer these features for the most part from past experience, simple monetary rules such as those proposed by Friedman make the task easier.[26]

NOTES

1. See, for instance, the recent work on the subject by Stanley Fischer, Edmund S. Phelps, James Tobin, and others.

2. See, for example, the discussions in Kevin D. Hoover, "Two Types of Monetarism," *Journal of Economic Literature*, March 1984, pp. 58–76; Frank Hahn, *Money and Inflation* (Oxford: Blackwell, 1982); James Tobin, "The Monetarist Counter-Revolution Today—An Appraisal," *Economic Journal*, March 1981, pp. 29–42.

3. George Macesich, *Monetarism: Theory and Policy* (New York: Praeger Publishers, 1983), pp. 155–158.

4. For a discussion of a number of these empirical results see *ibid*, pp. 152–158.

5. Milton Friedman, "The Role of Monetary Policy," *American Economic Review*, 158, no. 2 (1968): 1–17; Edmund S. Phelps, "Money-Wage Dynamics and Labor-Market Equilibrium," *Journal of Political Economy*, August 1968, pp. 678–711.

6. See, for instance, Robert E. Lucas, Jr., "Tobin and Monetarism: A Review Article," *Journal of Economic Literature*, June 1981, pp. 558–567.

7. See, for instance, George Macesich, *The Politics of Monetarism: Its Historical and Institutional Development* (Totowa, N.J.: Rowman and Allanheld, 1984).

8. See, for instance, Milton Friedman and Anna J. Schwartz, *Monetary Trends in the United States and the United Kingdom: Their Relation to Income, Prices, and Interest Rates, 1867–1975* (Chicago: University of Chicago Press, 1982).

9. For a more detailed discussion of this point, see Hoover, "Two Types of Monetarism," pp. 61–62.

10. See Macesich, *The Politics of Monetarism*, for a discussion of the on-going debate over rules versus discretionary authority. For

the new classical view, see Robert E. Lucas, Jr., "Rules, Discretion, and the Role of the Economic Advisor," in *Rational Expectations and Economic Policy*, ed. Stanley Fischer (Chicago: University of Chicago Press, 1980), pp. 199–220; and Robert E. Lucas, *Studies in Business Cycle Theory* (Oxford: Blackwell, 1981).

11. John M. Culbertson, *Macroeconomic Theory and Stabilization Policy* (New York: McGraw-Hill, 1968), p. 545.

12. *Ibid*, p. 545. Culbertson puts it well when he writes:

A basic difficulty with undefined policy systems . . . is that since the policies to be followed are uncertain, they may prove to be disastrously inappropriate. Such policy systems are risky. The intellectual difficulty of this proponent of discretionary policy formation is a real one. If the policy matters, then certain correct choices must be made, which may be that power must reside in those particular men who will make the correct decisions—but in a context in which the correct choices themselves are asserted to be incapable of being defined (since it is the basis of rejection of defined policy systems). Inevitably, it seems the approach implies the existence of an elite or priestly class that promises to accomplish the indefinable. *Ibid.*, p. 535.

13. *Ibid.*, p. 534. For instance, John K. Galbraith attributes the lack of "success" of monetarism in the United States and Great Britain to difficulties at three levels. There is, according to Galbraith, first, the difficulty as to what is "money"; there is, second, that what a central bank elects to call *money* cannot either in quantity or velocity be controlled; there is, third, the certainty that efforts at vigorous control will substitute for the problem of inflation the alternative of high unemployment, recession, or depression, and disaster for those industries that depend on borrowed money. In effect, monetarism that places its sole confidence in stabilizing the growth of once "esoteric monetary aggregate" to the exclusion of other concerns is a prescription for calamity. John K. Galbraith, "Up From Monetarism and Other Wishful Thinking," *New York Review of Books*, August 13, 1981, pp. 27–32.

14. Macesich, *The Politics of Monetarism*, Chapter 7.

15. Milton Friedman, "Monetary Policy: Theory and Practice," *Journal of Money, Credit and Banking*, February 1982, p. 98.

16. William McChesny Martin to Milton Friedman, April 17, 1969.

17. Friedman, "Monetary Policy," p. 106.

18. Ibid.

19. Robert E. Weintraub, "Congressional Supervision of Monetary Policy," *Journal of Monetary Economics*, April 1978, pp. 341–62. See also Robert D. Auerbach, *Money, Banking and Financial Markets* (New York: Macmillan, 1982), pp. 362–64; Thomas M. Hav-

rilesky, "The Economist's Corner: The Politicization of Monetary Policy," *The Banker's Magazine*, Spring 1975, pp. 101–4. In fact, Havrilesky writes:

The politicization of the Federal Reserve System is rather an accomplished fact. With monetary policy so hamstrung by the political constraints and regulations of its own leadership, it is no surprise that the Federal Reserve spokesmen appeal to the interference for wage and price controls and continually repeat the tired litany which attacks economic theory for its lack of (political) realism, and thereby defends its own obscurantism. (P. 104.)

See also Nathaniel Beck, "Presidential Influence on the Federal Reserve in the 1970's," *American Journal of Political Science*, August 1982, pp. 415–45.

20. On the ownership issue and the Fed's independence, see George Macesich, "Stock and the Federal Reserve System," U.S. Congress, House, Subcommittee on Domestic Finance of the Committee on Banking and Currency, *Compendium on Monetary Policy Guidelines and Federal Reserve Structure*, 90th Cong., 2d sess. (Washington, D.C.: U.S. Government Printing Office, December 1968), pp. 454–57; and Macesich, "Central Banking, Monetary Policy and Economic Activity," ibid., pp. 437–54.

21. George Macesich, *The Politics of Monetarism*, pp. 94–104.

22. *New Monetary Control Procedures*, Federal Reserve Staff Study, vols. 1 and 2 (Washington D.C.: Board of Governors of the Federal Reserve System, February 1982). For a review of these studies, see Stephen M. Goldfeld, "New Monetary Control Procedures," *Journal of Money, Credit and Banking*, February 1982, pp. 148–55. Seel also JMCB Debate "Is the Federal Reserve's Monetary Control Policy Misdirected?" *Journal of Money, Credit and Banking*, February 1982, pp. 119–47.

23. Friedman, "Monetary Policy: Theory and Practice," p. 124.

24. Macesich, *Politics of Monetarism*, pp. 118–121.

25. For a succinct discussion of these and related issues, see Culbertson, *Macroeconomic Theory and Stabilization Policy*, pp. 410–11; A. Downs, *Inside Bureaucracy* (Boston: Little, Brown, 1967); H. G. Johnson, "Problems of Efficiency in Monetary Management," *Journal of Political Economy*, October 1968, pp. 971–90; Keith Hebeson and John F. Chant, "Bureaucratic Theory and the Choice of Central Bank Goals: The Case of the Bank of Canada," *Journal of Money, Credit and Banking*, May 1973, pp. 637–55; P. Selznik, "Foundations of the Theory of Organizations," *American Sociological Review* 13 (1948), reprinted as F. E. Emery, ed., *Systems Thinking* (Harmondsworth: Penguin Books, 1969); O. F. Williamson, *The Economics of Discre-*

tionary Behavior: Managerial Objectives in a Theory of the Firm (Chicago: Markham Publishing Company, 1964); Albert Breton and Ronald Wintrobe, *The Logic of Bureaucratic Conduct* (Cambridge: Cambridge University Press, 1982).

26. Lucas, "Rules, Discretion, and the Role of the Economic Advisor," p. 199.

CHAPTER 5

Methodological Issue

Although the new classicals accept the Friedman monetarists' position on the policy issues and supporting empirical evidence, they do not always travel identical theoretical paths. The new classicals wish to analyze economic dynamics with the rational expectations hypothesis. Their approach is to collapse the long run into the short run and thereby appeal to the other tenets of their doctrine.[1]

This is not the approach favored by the Friedman monetarists. They prefer the Marshallian approach and its distinction between the market short run and long run periods for dealing with economic dynamics.

In applying the rational expectations hypothesis it is common, write Friedman and Schwartz,

to proceed on two assumptions: (1) that participants in whatever market is considered have "correct" estimates of the probability distribution of outcomes (itself something that is difficult or impossible to define objectively), that on the average are correct; and (2) that errors of forecast in successive time units are uncorrelated.[2]

An example of what this means is provided by the American silver episode during the closing years of the nineteenth century. This episode, Friedman and Schwartz write, is especially instructive with respect to the proper interpretation of the recently popular theory of rational expectations. . . . [It] brings out sharply the difficulty of giving a precise meaning to the first assumption, and ambiguity of the "time unit" for the second assumption. For that episode, the relevant time unit is about twenty years—so that averaging out may take a long time. Our analysis [U.S. and U.K. monetary trends and their relation to outcome, prices and interest rates from 1867 to 1975] gives one example: The real yield on nominal assets matches the real yield on physical assets only for the whole century of our data covered.[3]

Not surprisingly, they conclude that the hypothesis is not the "open sesame to unravelling the riddle of dynamic change that some of its more enthusiastic proponents make it out to be."[4]

THE CHICAGO APPROACH

The Friedman monetarist approach is, of course, in keeping with the traditional Chicago approach to economic research. This approach long antedates the new classical emphasis on rational expectations. To be sure, the rational expectations hypothesis is very much in the spirit of the Chicago approach to economics—for example, competitive markets must clear, decision makers must optimize, money illusion must be absent. It is thus not surprising that rational expectations and the new classicals have thus far had a favorable reception in Chicago.[5] Other approaches, however, can accommodate rational expectations, as indeed Tobin points out.[6]

In the Chicago tradition, the money supply and its impact upon a competitive economy, both in response to shocks with various adjustment lags and in long-run stationary equilibrium, provide much that is important in the "macro" sense in which that term is used elsewhere. Autonomous macroeconomics is rejected by the Chicago tradition. Macrodynamics, on the other hand, is compatible with this tradition so long as stable relationships involve continuous individual optimization.[7] What this tradition rejects is a macrostatics with one of the variables indicating resource utilization and implying at equilibrium a less than full utilization of resources and thus the availability of free resources that monetary authorities can obtain through the manipulation of the money supply. This view also is readily accepted by the new classicals.

In the Chicago tradition it is, for the most part, prices, quantities, and wealth that best serve the analyst and not simply self-reports of participants in the economic process. Reder discusses this tradition under the rubric of "Tight Prior Equilibrium" or TP, which serves here in our discussion.[8] Reder's TP

is rooted in the hypothesis that decision makers so allocate the resources under their control that there is no alternative allocation such that any one decision maker could have his expected utility increased without a reduction occurring in the expected utility of at least one other decision maker. . . . For Chicago and non-Chicago economists alike this is a definition of Pareto optimality, which may or may not be associated with a model that yields particular testable hypotheses, depending upon whether certain further assumptions are made. Chicago economists typically make these other assumptions while others often refuse to do so. . . .[9]

The further assumptions that Chicago economists make, according to Reder, are the following:

(1) *most* individual transactors treat the prices of all goods and services that they buy and sell, as independent of the quantities that they transact;
(2) the prices at which individuals *currently agree* to transact are market clearing prices that are consistent with optimization by all decision makers;
(3) information bearing on prices and quantities of all things bought and sold, present and future, is acquired in the quantity that makes its marginal cost equal to price; i.e., information is treated like any other commodity;
(4) neither monopoly nor governmental action (through taxation or otherwise) affects relative prices or quantities sufficiently to prevent either marginal products or compensation of identical resources from being approximately equal in all uses.[10]

It is, of course, understood that none of the assumptions Reder lists are believed to hold exactly. They are taken simply as a first approximation. Random disturbances do occur, influencing tastes and preferences, techniques, information and the character of goods and services, thus influencing in a transitory manner the above assumptions. These random disturbances, however, lend themselves to a stochastic counterpart to the exact or nonstochastic competitive general equilibrium model with the property that if for all commodities the expected price and expected quantity are treated as proxies for the corresponding price and quantity in the exact model then all propositions concerning partial derivatives with respect to quantities and of quantities with respect to prices in the exact model will hold also in the stochastic model so long as we substitute "expected price" for price and "expected quantity" for quantity.[11]

These propositions about partial derivatives are, according to the Chicago TP view presented by Reder, the only valid propositions concerning economic theory. Accordingly, there exist no empirical relationships among prices, quantities and disturbances other than those that are counterparts to the exact general equilibrium model. This does not necessarily mean that economic theory is the *sine qua non* for explaining all relationships between prices and quantities. The character and nature of the disturbance will also dictate the effectiveness and power of economic theory in any given analysis.

Moreover, mutual independence of all disturbances and each disturbance with respect to each expected price and quantity is sufficient to satisfy TP requirements. This assumption is really not necessary, according to Reder, since any of a wide variety of patterns of offsetting covariations will do the job. Furthermore, it is only in the long run and under stationary conditions that mutual independence can be assumed to hold. This is understandable since current demand and supply schedules themselves may be and usually are under the influence of past errors, imperfect forecasts, long-term contracts, past durable asset aquisitions, and various leads and lags.

In any case, in empirical work it is usually assumed by TP practitioners that, in the absence of evidence to the contrary, one can treat observed prices and quantities as good approximations to their long-run competitive values. This is called by

Reder the "good approximation assumption." This assumption makes it possible for researchers to abstract from the effects of transitory market imperfections that result in resource misallocation and underutilization of resources, and thus permits the analyst to treat observed input prices as measures of the opportunity cost of the imputed output associated with their use.

"The good approximation assumption" is characteristic of most empirical work in the Chicago tradition. This assumption, however, is not tested directly as to its descriptive accuracy as we shall discuss. It is instead treated as a maintained hypothesis and applied using the findings as a test of TP. Thus Reder writes that "in the applications of human capital theory, one does not usually measure the marginal productivity of labor directly, but assumes it to be equal to the relevant wage rate at each moment and estimates investment in training from the earnings profile."[12]

In the Chicago tradition there is a strong tendency to gauge research results against the implications of price theory. Inconsistency of empirical results with implications of theory and/or behavior that are not implied by theory requires further action along one or more avenues. First, data may be wrong and so should be reexamined; second, the variables are improperly defined and/or they are in need of augmentation; third, the theory must be adjusted to take account of behavior inconsistent with the rationality assumption by one or more economic agents; fourth, the empirical results may themselves be placed on the agenda for further research. The Chicago tradition focuses on the first and second possibilities, and if no resolution is found, moves to the fourth possibility with little regard for the third possibility. Other traditions would, presumably, focus on the third possibility as well.

It is the short run where existing stocks of assets and contracts may not be optimum that the good approximation assumption and TP of the Chicago view run into special problems. Most Chicago economists recognize these short run problems when observed wage and prices are sticky. When prices and wages are less than fully flexible and subject to the quantity constraints of past outlays and contracts, all markets will not .clear as envisioned by TP. There is a need to reconcile these issues with the maintained hypothesis of continuous optimization.

In fact, these long-standing empirical anomalies are an illustration of our fourth possibility discussed above. They are high on the empirical research agenda in Chicago and elsewhere. Much of the work on search and information and contracts is devoted to these items on the research agenda.[13] There is, in essence, a singular resistance to institutional or ethical explanations for the behavior of prices and quantities that are incompatible with the assumption of optimization as of the moment of decision making.

The Friedman monetarists stress that both prices and wages respond slowly to changes in aggregate demand. Indeed, most Chicago economists usually assume that in the long run wages are sufficiently flexible to equate the demand and supply of labor. This is in marked contrast, for instance, to the conventional view, which argues that even during periods of prosperity there is usually a large pool of workers who cannot find employment. This is a consequence, so the argument goes, of the tendency for the growth of the labor force to exceed the growth of aggregate demand and the long-run inflexibility of wages for institutional or ethical reasons.

The Chicago view of the economic system assumes that competition is a major force in the economy. This view insists on the usefulness of competitive theory as an approach to understanding economic activity. Critics reject the results of competitive price theory analyses on the grounds that the theory's assumptions of individual choice and maximizing behavior are unrealistic. Friedman's reply in his essay entitled "The Methodology of Positive Economics" is that the test of a good theory is "its ability to predict much from little" rather than the realism of its assumptions.[14]

FRIEDMAN ON MARSHALL, COURNOT, AND WALRAS

Friedman is essentially Marshallian in his approach to economic theory and its application. To Friedman, Marshallian economics is not just a set of theories or hypotheses to explain the working of a market or economic system. For Friedman, and others who share his views, Marshallian economics is much more. It is a method or a framework within which to operate. In this view, an economic system is one of perpetual change and evolution. In his *Principles of Economics*, Alfred Marshall (1842–1924) expounded his notion of continuing adjustment. Equilibrium is shown as something that is constantly being sought, but never attained, because new factors are always intruding to change the direction of the adjustment process. How should such complexities be handled? Simplification is clearly necessary.

Marshall was much influenced by John Stuart Mill's work and he credits Antoine Augustin Cournot (1801–1877) with having helped him form his ideas. Cournot's insights into the complex nature of economic phenomena, and especially of coming to grips with their empirical nature, are also favorably quoted by Friedman.[15] Focusing on Chapter 11 of Cournot's *Researches*, Friedman thus quotes the following from Cournot:

So far we have studied how, for each commodity by itself, the law of demand in connection with the conditions of production of that commodity, determines the price of it and regulates the incomes of its producers. We considered as given and invariable the prices of other commodities and the incomes of other producers; but in reality, the economic system is a whole of which all the parts are connected and react on each other. An increase in the income of the producers of commodity A will affect the demand for commodities B, C, etc., and the incomes of their producers, and by its reaction, will involve a change in the demand for commodity A. It seems, therefore, as if, for a complete and rigorous solution of the problems relative to some parts of the economic system, it were indispensable to take the entire system into consideration. But this would surpass the powers of mathematical analysis and of our practical methods of calculation, even if the values of all the constants could be assigned to them numerically" (p. 127 Cournot's *Researches*).[16]

Drawing on Cournot's problem in discussing the Walrasian general equilibrium approach to economic interdependence, Friedman writes:

It is Walras' great and living achievement to have constructed a mathematical system displaying in considerable detail precisely the interrelationships emphasized by Cournot. Did he thereby show Cournot to be wrong in supposing that the task surpassed the powers of mathematical analysis? I believe not. For there is a fundamental, if subtle, difference between the task Cournot outlined and the task Walras accomplished; an understanding of the difference is essential to an assessment of both the positive contribution of Walras and the limitations to that contribution; and failure to recognize the difference seems to me a primary source of confusion in economics. It is clear from Cournot's references to "practical methods of calculation" and to the assignment of numerical values to constants that the "rigorous solutions" he had in mind was not a solution "in principle" but a numerical solution to a specific problem. His goal was an analysis that would, given the relevant statistical material, yield specific answers to specific empirical questions, such as the effects of a specified tax on a specified product; answers that could be confronted by observation and confirmed or contradicted. And surely there can be little doubt that a "complete and rigorous solution" of this kind does "surpass the powers of mathematical analysis and of our practical methods of calculation" even today despite the enormous advances in methods of calculation. Cournot was quite right that *for his problem* a "complete and rigorous" solution was out of the question, that the thing to do was, "while maintaining a certain kind of approximation . . . to carry on . . . a useful analysis.[17]

In the same spirit the important distinction between Walras and Marshall, argues Friedman, is in the fact that Marshall sought "an engine for the discovery of concrete truth."[18]

What then are the principal elements in the Marshallian "engine of analysis for the discovery of truth?" Two are paramount. One concerns the breakdown of complex interrelationships, the other the handling of time.

Consider the first element. Marshallian economics is frequently referred to as partial equilibrium analysis and often contrasted to general equilibrium, which was presented by Leon Walras (1834–1910).[19] In a very broad sense this is correct. Usually, when Marshall spoke of a market, a demand, or a supply, he had in mind the market for a particular consumers' good or production factor. His demand schedule reflected a functional relationship between the price of the good or the production factor and the quantity offered for sale. This is not to say that Marshall ignored the interrelationships that existed between a particular market and price and other markets and prices in the economy as a whole. Frequently, he used the assumption *ceteris paribus*, that is, other things remain the same. He argued that such and such would be the price, all other demands, supplies, and prices remaining the same. This assumption, of course, is often an unreal one. Thus the response in sales of a particular good or service may be different when the price of a substitute is very low than when the price of a near substitute is relatively dear. The response may also be different, for instance, when the price of one substitute alters than when the price of another does so.

The alternative to the Marshallian approach, according to some economists, including the new classicals, in a system of complicated equations of the Walrasian system that is sharply criticized by Friedman. Indeed, according to Friedman, the Walrasian system is not really an alternative at all. Thus he writes:

Walras solved a different, though no less important problem. He emptied Cournot's problem of its empirical content and produced a "complete and rigorous" solution "in principle," making no pretense that it could be used directly in numerical calculations. His problem is the problem of form, not of content: of displaying an idealized picture of the economic system, not of constructing an engine for analyzing concrete problems. His achievement cannot but impress the reader with its beauty, its grandeur, its architectonic structure; it would verge on the ludicrous to describe it as a demonstration how to calculate the numerical solution to a numerically specified set of equations. The difference is brought out clearly by the further developments along Walras' line that have been—and rightly—regarded as improvements in his system. These have all consisted in making the system still more general and elegant, in eliminating empirically specializing assumptions. The clearest example is, of course, in the theory of production: Walras assumed constant coefficients of production. The recent reintroduction of the assumption of constant coefficients of production in connection with input-output analysis has not been a further development of Walras' pure theory. It has rather been an attempt—so far largely unsuccessful—to use Walrasian constructs in solving Cournot's problem.[20]

In Friedman's view (and, again, most economists agree)

economics not only requires a framework for organizing our ideas it requires also ideas to be organized. We need the right kind of language; we also need something to say. Substantive hypotheses about economic phenomena of the kind that were the goal of Cournot are an essential ingredient of a fruitful and meaningful economic theory. Walras has little to contribute in this direction; for this we must turn to other economists, notably, of course, to Alfred Marshall.[21]

Consider now the second important element in Marshallian economics—the handling of time. To make it amenable to inquiry, Marshall broke time down into a series of planning periods, which were associated with the degree of fixity of the factors under control. For purposes of exposition, he identified three time periods with respect to production. First, there was a period that was too short for production to take place. In this period, Marshall said, a temporary equilibrium was reached in the market. Allowing for such factors as storage and withdrawals from storage, and the desire to avoid "spoiling the market" by making sales at prices lower than they could afford to accept over a longer period, the price of a good in this short period would be that at which the existing supply could find buyers.

The second period was one that Marshall referred to as the short-period normal. It was a period long enough for production to take place with the aid of existing skill, equipment, and organization, but insufficiently long for the supply of these facilities to be altered.

The third period was the long-period normal, sufficiently long for all production factors, aside from land, to be altered in supply. In this period, all costs other than the rent of land became variable.

Marshall spoke of the short-period normal as being a "few months or a year," and the long-period normal as being "several years," but he said there was "no hard and sharp line of division" between the two periods. He also suggested that as a "general rule" the shorter the time period the greater our focus on demand as a determinant of price and the longer the period the more important are supply and the costs of production on price.[22] Aside from the element of time he did not assign priority to either demand or supply as determining price. Instead he used a simile and spoke of a number of balls "resting against one another in a basin" in recognition of the possibility that there may be more than two elements affecting value (the demand for a good and the supply of the same good). Indeed the "balls-in-a-basin" illustration might well have served Walras with regard to his own system.

This analysis of time leads us into a central aspect of the theoretical structure of Marshallian economics. This concerns what Marshall called the theory of value, which is now called the theory of relative price determination. The basic argument is that relative prices and changes in them are determined by the demand and supply conditions in different markets and the changes in these conditions. These are the so-called laws of supply and demand so often referred to in economic discussions.

The Marshallian vision of the economic system is one in which changing demand and supply conditions in the various commodity, factor, and financial markets are continuously altering the set of relative prices. Decision makers adjust their behavior accordingly. These adjustments are made according to the principle of substitution. Decision makers are assumed to be individual welfare maximizers—that is, they take actions and respond to economic circumstances that will, in their subjective judgment, maximize the welfare of the unit they represent.

Any change in relative prices will make existing prices nonoptimal and hence will encourage substitution. Consumers and/or producers will attempt to lower the use of a product and/or factor whose relative price has increased. The principle of substitution is, in effect, the mechanism by which the economy adjusts to changes in the underlying economic structure, and the signaling system for this mechanism to operate is the system of relative prices. Critical to Marshallian economics is a system of price flexibility that conveys information about the ever changing economic environment.

Keynes's criticism that in the "real world" price flexibility is an illusion and hence the burden of adjustment to changing circumstances normally falls on output and employment brings us to Marshall's monetary theory. The prototype of Friedman's monetary work is to be found in Marshall's monetary economics, including the analysis of the demand for money as a stable function of real income or wealth.

THE NEW CLASSICALS AND FRIEDMAN

In the Marshallian spirit Friedman preserves the distinction between the short run and long run. The new classicals, on the other hand, collapse the long run into the short run. This has been noted as the principal methodological difference between the Friedman monetarists and the new classicals.[23] In the Chicago tradition both agree that economic agents are optimizers. For Friedman and others with similar views it is impossible to document in detail the optimization process for reasons discussed by Cournot.

In any case, a satisfactory approach to the complexities of economic interdependence raised by Cournot is to partition a given problem under review along Marshallian lines into the short run and long run, as does Friedman. Thus if one is interested in long-run behavior, it is legitimate to assume that even if short-run behavior of economic agents differs from long-run behavior, they are still optimizing under unspecified constraints. In Friedman's view we can be confident that agents do their best in optimizing even though we cannot specify how they do so. For their part, however, the new classicals require that we specify precisely the informational limits that constrain the agents if we are to understand their behavior at all.

The Marshallian approach is used by Friedman and others as an avenue for conducting economic research in the face of the empirical complexities discussed by Cournot. It does not eliminate such complexities; they are always before the Friedman-type analyst. The new classicals apparently do not consider the Cournot issues as cause for skepticism. On the contrary, they are optimistic that the Walrasian approach of fully specifying the optimization problem that agents face can indeed be carried out.[24].

Friedman typically focuses on the long run since much more information is available than for the short run. For instance, evidence supports the existence of a stabler long-run demand for money. This is also underscored in the long-run stable relation between money and prices as well as in their long and variable leads and lags.

As Hoover correctly points out, the new classical approach is Walrasian.[25] As noted above, the method is to impose a fully specified theory on the data and to use the rational expectation hypothesis to solve the problem that the future is unknown. In effect, the Marshallian long run is collapsed into the short run.[26]

Differences between Friedman and the new classicals also turn on the important issues of risk and uncertainty. For many years Frank Knight at the University of Chicago discussed and developed the useful concepts of risk and uncertainty to economics.[27] Since economic agents are incapable of knowing the future they are subject to error. Some errors are of an insurable nature, which Knight terms "risk." The other category of errors are those not insurable, which he places in a category called "uncertainty." Friedman considers the categories and their distinction as important. Accordingly, an agent's ignorance of future events that is quantifiable is "risk" and that which is not is "uncertainty." The long run is thus characterized by risk and, in effect, forecast errors are not correlated. The short run, on the other hand, is characterized by uncertainty and forecast errors are correlated. Friedman makes use of these categories in a number of studies.[28]

For their part, the new classicals argue that uncertainty has no place in economic analysis.[29] Given their Walrasian position and collapsing the long run into the short run, this is understandable. In a fully specified model, uncertainty is a residual about which we know nothing. As a consequence, it cannot be analyzed. The only departure from the dynamic path of the economy, which is a fully optimizing path, is by no more than a serially uncorrelated error—categorized as risk.

Can these differences between Friedman and the new classicals be viewed as a departure by the latter from the received Chicago tradition or perhaps as a return to pre-Friedman Chicago? It can be argued that a tradition more amenable to the new classical view did exist at one time in Chicago. Reder, for instance, tells us that before the arrival of Frank Knight and his student Henry Simons the intellectual style of arriving Chicago Ph.D.s did not differ significantly from those elsewhere.[30] Knight had many admirers among the student body at Chicago, including this writer and such people as Milton Friedman, George Stigler, and Allan Wallis. The last three are important for setting forth the now familiar Chicago view.

The Chicago tradition does indeed owe much to Knight and, as Reder puts it, to the "Knight affinity group" whose principal members also include Rose Director Friedman, Aaron Director, and Henry Simons.[31] Ironically, Jacob Viner was probably closer than Knight to what is now regarded as the Chicago view. Thus Viner focused on money, international trade, and on empirical, though not necessarily on mathematical-quantitative, research. For various reasons Viner never managed to attract the following that Knight did.[32]

In the Chicago tradition, Reder also places Robert Lucas as a principal exponent of the new classical economics and its Walrasian methodology. He writes that "Frank Knight, Jacob Viner, Henry Simons, and Lloyd Mints can be considered precursors of Friedman, George Stigler, Gary Becker, and Robert Lucas."[33] There is little doubt about the first three. Lucas, however, does not appear to share similar theoretical and methodological views for reasons already discussed.

The new classicals are thus not type II monetarists as Tobin and others argue. In spite of similar policy prescriptions there are important theoretical differences firmly lodged in methodology between the new classicals and Friedman monetarists. The former are Walrasian while the latter are Marshallian. The former are much more optimistic than the latter in providing a solution to Cournot's problem discussed by Friedman. In their euphoria to distinguish their product the new classicals may be well advised not to confuse pure theory with applied theory.[34]

NOTES

1. See Kevin D. Hoover, "Two Types of Monetarism," *Journal of Economic Literature*, March 1984, pp. 58–76.

2. Milton Friedman and Anna J. Schwartz, *Monetary Trends in the United States and United Kingdom: Their Relation to Income, Prices and Interest Rates, 1867–1975*. (Chicago: University of Chicago Press, 1982), p. 630.

3. *Ibid.*

4. *Ibid.*

5. Melvin W. Reder, "Chicago Economics: Permanence and Change," *Journal of Economic Literature*, March 1982, pp. 1–38.

6. James Tobin, *Asset Accumulation and Economic Activity: Reflections on Contemporary Macroeconomic Theory* (Chicago: University of Chicago Press, 1980).

7. Reder, "Chicago Economics," p. 19.

8. *Ibid.*, pp. 1–38.

9. *Ibid.*, p. 11.

10. *Ibid.*

11. *Ibid.*, p. 12.

12. *Ibid.*, p. 13.

13. See George J. Stigler, "The Economics of Information," *Journal of Political Economy*, June 1961, pp. 213–25; J. Hirshleifer and John G. Riley, "The Analytics of Uncertainty and Information—An Expository Survey," *Journal of Economic Literature*, December 1979, pp. 1375–1421.

14. Milton Friedman, ed. *Essays in Positive Economics* (Chicago: University of Chicago Press, 1953), pp. 3–43.

15. A. A. Cournot, *Recherches sur les principes mathematiques de la théori des Richesses* (Researches into the mathematical principles of the theory of wealth), trans. Nathaniel T. Bacon (New York, 1897; originally published in 1838); Milton Friedman, "Leon Walras and His Economic System," *The American Economic Review*, December 1955, pp. 903–4.

16. Friedman, "Leon Walras and His Economic System," p.

17. *Ibid.*, p. 904.

18. Milton Friedman, "The Marshallian Demand Curve," *Journal of Political Economy*, December 1949, pp. 463–95; reprinted in his *Essays in Positive Economics*, pp. 47–99.

19. See Leon Walras, *Elements of Pure Economics*, translated by William Jaffé, published for the American Economic Association and the Royal Economic Society (Homewood, Ill.: Richard Irwin, 1954);

and review by Friedman, "Leon Walras and His Economic System," pp. 900–909.

20. Friedman, "Leon Walras and His Economic System," pp. 904–5.

21. *Ibid.*, p. 908.

22. Alfred Marshall, *Principles of Economics*, 8th Edition. (London: Macmillan, 1920), Book III, Chapters 1, 2, and 3.

23. See Hoover, "Two Types of Monetarism," p. 71.

24. *Ibid.* See, in particular, Thomas J. Sargent, "Beyond Demand and Supply Curves in Macroeconomics," *The American Economic Review*, May 1982, pp. 382–89.

25. Hoover, "Two Types of Monetarism," p. 71.

26. *Ibid.*

27. Frank Knight, *Risk Uncertainty and Profit* (London: London School of Economics, 1937).

28. See, for instance, Friedman and Schwartz, *Monetary Trends in the United States and the United Kingdom.*

29. Robert E. Lucas, Jr., "Understanding Business Cycles," in *Stabilization of the Domestic and International Economy*, ed. Karl Brunner and Allan H. Meltzer, Carnegie-Rochester Conference Series, Vol. 5 (Amsterdam: North Holland, 1977), pp. 7–30.

30. Reder, "Chicago Economics," p. 5.

31. *Ibid.*, pp. 6–7.

32. *Ibid.*

33. *Ibid.*, p. 3.

34. See, for instance, the discussion of related issues in Friedman, "Leon Walras and His Economic System," pp. 900–909.

CHAPTER 6

Business Cycle Issue

TWO VIEWS

Business cycles have long been an integral part of modern and interdependent economies. Much has been written about their characteristics and behavior, especially since the nineteenth century and the upsurge in world industrial development.[1] The new classical approach, for its part, finds it extremely difficult to come to grips with the business cycle issue.

This is not surprising. Given their Walrasian method and their insistence that no unexploited profit opportunities exist, why do rational economic agents not see it in their interest to eliminate economic fluctuations? There is recognition of this issue on the part of the new classicals as the central problem in macroeconomics.[2] How, indeed, can business cycles be triggered by unanticipated monetary-fiscal shocks without at the same time violating the assumption of continuous competitive equilibrium and the absence of unexploited profit opportunities?

According to one view economic agents have imperfect information; as a consequence they make unsystematic mistakes in the face of monetary shocks.[3] Moreover, agents make decisions on the basis of these mistakes. They expand output and if they are ignorant of the monetary shocks' transient nature they increase investment to adjust the capital stock to an increase in demand. Given rational expectations, economic agents soon learn of their mistakes. They are, nevertheless, now faced with a higher capital stock and a changed environment. Since the capital stock is higher than they desire, they also reduce investment to reduce the capital stock to its optimal level. Thus a cycle is generated even in the absence of further monetary shocks.

In the new classical view of business cycles, prices also cycle since the intitial money supply increase produces a greater than otherwise increase in their pace. The increased capacity, once it comes on line, will retard the rate of price increase below the steady-state rate until the optimal capital stock is restored. The other real magnitudes, such as employment and output, connected with the agents' plans to their decisions about the capital stock and investment will also cycle. Accordingly, economic agents do not make persistent mistakes. Even when they act optimally, however, their mistakes leave persistent consequences.

In short, the essential idea is to start from a neoclassical growth model.[4] Assume steady-state certainty in which the money supply, prices, and real quantities grow at constant rates. To set the cycle off one assumes uncertainty and in particular an unanticipated increase in the money supply, which agents first perceive as an increase in demand. They expand output and investment only to find that they are mistaken in their initial perception. The capital produced by their erroneous investment nonetheless endures. They are thus stuck in a changed economic environment. However, the underlying premise of competitive general equilibrium, with flexible prices continuously clearing all markets, casts doubt on this version of the new classical business cycle model.

Thanks to their Marshallian method, Friedman monetarists' premise of continuously clearing markets provides no difficulties to their view of the business cycle. Since their focus is on the long run they are not encumbered with the necessity of knowing the short-run details of economic processes. It is sufficient in their view to summarize cyclical behavior as short-run adjustment toward the Marshallian long-run equilibrium, which itself may be moving.

The process is illustrated in the treatment of business cycles by Friedman and Schwartz in *Monetary History of the U.S.* and *Monetary Trends*.[5] In these studies it is assumed that the economy is in long-run equilibrium before and after a monetary shock. General properties of the economic dynamics are then deduced that must hold if the economy is to move from one long-run equilibrium to another. The analysis does not contain a full specification of the economic agents' economic environment that is required by the new classicals. To Friedman, the problem posed by economic dynamics can be usefully divided up into Marshallian runs and analyzed accordingly. To the Walrasian new classicals such an approach is impossible since in their analysis the long run is telescoped into the short run. They are left casting about in the face of various theoretical problems and recalcitrant facts.

LESSONS FROM THE PAST

The new classicals cannot turn readily for guidance to the past. Some authors, nevertheless, are more suggestive than others. Adam Smith (1723–1790), for instance, has little to say on the issue.[6] Classical economics was pervaded by the assumption that market divergencies from long-run equilibrium prices gradually diminish until the equilibrium point is reached. Possibly this helps explain the lack of attention given in the classical writings to the problem of cyclical behavior, seen especially in the neglect of general booms and depressions.

Smith did come close to stating a business cycle theory in discussion of a well-regulated paper currency. It is not in scarcity of gold and silver, he argued, but in the difficulty that such people have in borrowing and that their creditors have in getting payment that one hears complaints of the scarcity of money. The cause of such a state of affairs is the "overtrading" of merchants who later find it impossible to repay. His solution is that merchants should be more prudent and use better judgment. They should not be provided more money to get them out of their difficulties.

It was James Maitland, eighth Earl of Lauderdale (1759–1839), a critic of Smith, who suggested a theory of business cycles that later writers picked up, including the new classical version discussed above. He suggested that in boom periods, capital goods may be constructed in excess of the subsequent demand for their products.

In general, involuntary unemployment and underemployment of resources is neglected in the mainstream of classical writings. Only Thomas Malthus (1766–1834), among acknowledged leaders of the classical school, gave much attention to it. Moreover, his treatment of the subject was regarded by other members of the classical group as something of a rebellion. It was Jean Baptiste Say (1767–1832) who stood for classical orthodoxy in this matter and not Malthus. The basis of the orthodox position was the classical emphasis on long-term phenomena. Indeed, in David Ricardo's (1772–1823) opinion, political economy, as it had been developed at that time, was a science of long-run tendencies and cycles were short-run phenomena that had no place in such a science.

Karl Marx (1818–1883) considered, among other things, the credit system in its relation to business activity. He argued that the extension of credit was based on production itself. Thus the granting of loans when finished goods were sold ("credit reflex") was assured. An interference with the "flow" and "reflex" of credit resulting from a delay in receiving payments, overstocked markets, or decline in prices, will result in credit ceasing to perform its function. In Marx's view, goods cannot be marketed and fixed capital will be underutilized.

This is similar to an idea expressed earlier by John Stuart Mill (1806–1873) and later more fully developed by others. It is that business declines are closely correlated with the circulation of money and changes in the volume of credit. These changes in turn are reflected in alternatives in the degree of liquidity of business assets.

William Stanley Jevons (1835–1882) in his studies of business cycles compiled a considerable amount of data and did pioneer work in the field of cycles. His study of price fluctuations, for instance, anticipated later work on the economic effects of price inflation. His theory of the relation of sunspots to business depressions may appear farfetched, but it was presented at a time in history when the bulk of the world was agricultural. Moreover, he does represent cycles as exogenous shocks to an otherwise stable system.

The influence of the monetary factor has been discussed even earlier by such writers as Thomas Attwood (1783–1856) and Thomas Joplin (1790–1847). Attwood and the "Birmingham" school believed that it was currency deflation that caused trade depression and advocated the issue of inconvertible paper money as a remedy. Joplin argued that booms and depressions can be attributed to monetary expansion and contraction. Moreover, Joplin underscored the relationship between internal credit and international gold flows—an issue later stressed by Marx and John Maynard Keynes.

The periodicity of business cycles was discussed by such writers as Clement Juglar (1819–1905). In fact, Joseph Schumpeter (1883–1950) later called Juglar's investigations in the periodicity of cycles of about a ten-year duration as "Juglar cycles." Juglar identified three cyclical phases—prosperity, crises, and liquidation—that have had important influence on later writers.

Schumpeter, in fact, went on to systematize cycles in his own work, which emphasized the influence of innovations in cycles. He identified three distinct series: (1) a Juglar cycle of about ten years in duration; (2) a shorter cycle, about four months long, which he called the Kitchin cycle, attributing its identity to its discoverer, Joseph Kitchin; and (3) a long cycle of about 50 years discovered by Nikolai Kondratieff. According to Schumpeter there are three Kitchin cycles to a Juglar cycle, and six Juglars to a Kondratieff.

Other writers who have contributed significantly to cyclical theories and observations at the beginning of the twentieth century include M. I. Tugan-Baranowsky (1865–1919), A. A. C. Spiethoff (1873–1957), and Gustav Cassel (1866–1945). Their theories are really supplementary to each other. Thus there is a rising cost trend as a business boom proceeds. Demand, however, does not rise to absorb the increase in output created by the new investment. The net effect of these two factors is to slow and bring the upswing in the cycle to an end.

Knut Wicksell's work on the interrelationship between the interest rate, price level, and volume of business activity provided the foundation for what was to become the Swedish School, which included such members as E. R. Lindahl, G. Myrdal, and B. G. Ohlin. Among their contributions is the distinction between anticipations (ex ante) and realizations (ex post). They point out that business decisions are based mainly on expectations. Investment takes place when it is anticipated that a profit can be earned. Savings, on the other hand, are made out of realized incomes adjusting themselves for ex post losses and profits. In their view, manipulation of the interest rate as discussed by Wicksell can leave only a limited effect on economic activity owing to the influence of other factors, including wages and innovations.

The relation of interest, prices, and economic activity discussed by Wicksell is similar to the much earlier work of Thomas Thorton (1760–1815) and Sir Josiah Child (1630–1699). The idea is, essentially, the distinction made between the market rate of interest for capital and the rate that represented the productivity at which additional capital can be employed in economic activity. When the market rate is below that of the productivity rate, economic agents will increase their capital investment. The resulting increase in demand for productive services will raise their price. As the investment of new capital goes forth, the price level rises and the output of goods and services and employment in the economy increases.

It was, however, Sir Ralph George Hawtrey (1879–1971) who examined the influence of lags between income and expenditure, and the effect of changes in the interest rate on the cost of holding business inventories. According to Hawtrey, on a cyclical upswing bank credit is expanded, but it is not immediately spent by those to whom it is lent so that consumers do not have the extra income that would otherwise be immediately generated. Once consumers do receive the added income they quickly spend it, raising the volume of money in circulation. This reduces the reserves in the banking system, causing a rise in interest rates, and discouraging the build up of inventories. This is important in understanding Kitchin cycles and National Bureau cycles in which inventory changes play a significant role.

Lloyd A. Metzler developed a version of inventory cycles focusing on the relationship over the cycle between sales, inventories, and output. The idea is that when an increase in demand occurs in a time of below-marginal prosperity, an early effect is to reduce inventories. In their attempts to bring up their inventories to sales, output increases to a higher level than can be maintained after these proportions have been reached. The result is a falling production and income and contracting demand.

Wesley Mitchell (1874–1948) at the National Bureau considered business cycles as oscillations, each stage of which developed out of what preceded it. At the bottom of a cycle, business operating costs included interest on capital are low, inventories have been reduced, invested funds are accumulating and bank reserves have increased. As a consequence the stage for recovery is established. Conversely, in a boom period bank credit is extended, interest and other business costs are rising, and inventories are large. These conditions set the stage for a decline in economic activity.

Mitchell's work focused on understanding cyclical phenomena and not so much on their cause. Subsequent work on cycles at the National Bureau went on to develop "leading statistical" series and "statistical indicators" of particular importance in economic forecasting studies. Of course, much work by Milton Friedman and Anna J. Schwartz is in the National Bureau tradition.

The onset of the Depression and its concomitant problems provided additional urgency to cyclical discussions. J. M. Keynes argued as the main cause of "crises" a sudden collapse in the marginal efficiency of capital brought about by changed expectations. Indeed the fall might be so severe as to negate any practical reduction in the rate of interest to stimulate investment.

Following Keynes, Sir Roy F. Harrod (1900–1978) accepted

the view that "full" employment could be achieved in the present if there is sufficient investment to create the income for factors of production that is needed to buy the consumer goods that are being produced. He notes, however, that the amount of investment sufficient to generate full employment now may indeed be too great later. Thus as new investment becomes productive the additional output may no longer bring a price with sufficient incomes to purchase it. The net effect may well be that full employment now simply means more unemployment later.

J. R. Hicks (1904–   ) developed cyclical models along Harrod's lines. A characteristic feature of Hicks's work is to combine the multiplier concept discussed by Keynes with that of the accelerator developed earlier by J. B. Clark (1847–1938). The multiplier refers to spending and respending of money and the accelerator to the dependence of new investment on the changes in the level of consumption.

On balance these theorists provide a more formal articulation to an idea going back to Malthus and Marx. This idea is that cycles are caused by the volume of investment outrunning demand. Each writer expresses one or more factors of a very complicated total picture. Accumulation of investment funds is underscored by some writers. Others notice increased spending. Anticipations and business climate are noted by still others. Some write of rising costs checking the upswing of the cycle, still others the importance of innovations, while some focus their attention on amplitudes and time sequences of cycles.

We have already noted the decline in the general level of prices during the perid from the 1870s to the 1890s in our reference to the studies by Friedman and Schwartz. It is useful to discuss briefly the views of some contemporary writers of that episode.

During the two decades of the period 1870–1890 cyclical booms became less pronounced and depressions more scarce than had been the case from 1850 to 1873, when much of the trading world was on the gold standard. The subsequent price declines evoked appeals from the agricultural sector and other debtor interests for relief. An official of the British government's Board of Trade, Sir Robert Giffen (1837–1910), argued correctly that the downward trend in prices was in fact the result of the operation of the quantity theory of money. Prices were declining because increases in the population of gold standard countries necessitated a concomitant increase in the supply of gold. Since the increase was not forthcoming, prices were declining. Giffen recommended the circulation of paper money and increased use of checks and deposits as means for increasing the money supply. In the 1880s gold was discovered in sufficient quantities in South Africa and by the turn of the century the price levels of gold standard countries were on the upswing.

Our discussion of the Chicago School did not take into account Professor James Laurence Laughlin (1850–1933), since he did not share completely its views. Laughlin taught economics at Harvard, Cornell, and Chicago. He also studied the period of the closing decades of the nineteenth century. He disagreed with the view of the quantity theory of money, arguing instead that credit came into existence and went out of existence in response to the varying needs of trade, so that the quantity of money is not independent of the volume of transactions to be undertaken. The problem with Laughlin's argument is that the creation of credit against goods cannot go on indefinitely unless there is no legal limit, such as percentage reserve requirements, that relates the volume of credit to the quantity of gold.

I have discussed elsewhere the importance of uncertainty and that on occasion even when a country is on the gold standard, internal events can have a significant impact on the money supply.[7] A case in point is the almost decade-long struggle for monetary supremacy by Jacksonian Democrats and supporters of the Second Bank of the United States. Some of the contemporary reviews attributed the direct "cause" of the rise in prices in 1834–1836 in the United States and subsequent difficulties to the operations of "speculators." Friends of the federal administration and supporters of the Second Bank freely exchanged acrimonious charges, each blaming the other for the country's economic plight. Others simply blamed all three—the speculators as well as the two contestants for monetary supremacy. All groups agreed that something was "wrong" with the money system of the country, but of course they disagreed with what that "something" was. For example, the federal government emphasized "monopoly" in banking, and sought to eliminate such "monopoly" by the removal of government deposits from the Second Bank of the United States and by the elimination of the Bank as a national institution. In addition, the government sought to institute a "hard currency" in the place of existing "bank rags" (bank notes). The supporters of the Second Bank, on the other hand, argued that the new method of handling government deposits accumulated in the Treasury by 1836. The distribution of this surplus in 1837, they argued, precipitated the crises in that year and the difficulties that followed. As a solution to the country's economic plight, they called for a recharter of the Second Bank, or a similar institution, the return of government deposits, and a "well-regulated" bank currency. The term "well-regulated" was usually interpreted to mean "according to the needs of trade."

For almost a decade the struggle for monetary supremacy continued, and, of course, so did the uncertainty about the ultimate outcome. In respect to the struggle for monetary supremacy, it is worth emphasizing the contrast between the arithmetic and the economics of the situation. The rapid rise in the internal stock of money, prices, and the physical volume of trade in the period from 1834 to 1836 was coincident with the general external expansion. Coupled with the external expansion was the substantial inflow into the United States of both short-term and long-term capital. Although the capital inflow varied, owing partly to the uncertainty created by the struggle for monetary supremacy, it did not cease completely with the difficulties of 1837, but continued into 1839. Under these external conditions, internal adjustments were required on the part of the United States. The only question is how. If, for example, banks expand or contract their deposits and notes in circulation, this is not, under the assumed conditions, the reason the money supply rises or falls—it is only the form that is taken by a rise or fall that would have occurred one way or another. This is the difference between the arithmetic and economics of a situation. Thus the withdrawal of government deposits from the Second Bank and the use of state banks as depositories for government funds may well have increased money, prices, and surplus in the Treasury, but only because external circumstances in the period required an internal expansion. As was indicated, this does not mean that internal disturbances cannot affect the money supply and prices; they can, but only insofar as they affect the conditions of external balance. It could be, for example, that the internal monetary expansion, coupled with the distribution of the surplus, threatened suspension. This, in turn, would have promoted a capital outflow that would be deflationary.

During the period of suspension, 1837–1838, the situation in the United States was different. Internal monetary changes affected the internal price level, and through it the exchange rate, so the price level was no longer rigidly linked to external price levels. Although to a first approximation the changes in the internal stock of money were determined by the requirements of external balance, the particular way in which changes in the stock of money were achieved reflected domestic monetary influences.

A parallel can be drawn between the above episode and the U.S. silver episode discussed by Friedman and Schwartz. Both are classic examples of uncertainty, and they underscore the utility and importance of Friedman's Marshallian approach and the limitations of the new classical Walrasian methodology.

It is difficult to give a precise meaning to the ambiguity of the time unit over which forecast errors are uncorrelated and identification of the subjective with the objective probability distribution. In the silver episode (1870s to 1890s) the time unit is about 20 years. In the 1830s–1840s struggle for monetary supremacy it is about 10 years.

THE NEW CLASSICAL VIEW IN RETROSPECT

The new classical view, which attempts to develop a general business cycle theory consistent with strict adherence to economic equilibrium, whereby individual economic agents pursue self-interest and markets continuously clear through relative price changes, leaves much to be desired. Unlike the monetarists' approach, the new classicals cannot draw upon adaptive expectations as an explanation for cyclical duration. In their view expectations are rational and free of any bias and subject to random error only. Insofar as they are predictable, monetary changes will be correctly anticipated with appropriate adjustment in prices and nominal variables. Accordingly, only random monetary shocks can lead to price surprises and miscalculations necessary to set off cyclical movements in real variables.

There are historical roots to efforts to explain the business cycle not as a contradiction but as part of equilibrium theory. This in fact is what Hayek attempted in the 1930s.[8] Subsequent interpretation, however, characterized his contribution as a theory of monetary disequilibrium and an unstable cumulative process with excessive credit causing distortions of relative prices and the structure of production.[9]

As we have discussed, in the basic equilibrium model of business cycles advanced by some new classical economists, random monetary shocks induce price misperceptions which induce wrong production decisions. The model assumes that prices other than those in one's own market are known to others only with a time lag of unspecified duration. Thus economic agents have full information only about their own operations. They have incomplete and lagging information about that of other agents as well as of such aggregates as the money supply and price level. Given an unexpected monetary shock manifested, for instance, by an acceleration in monetary growth, the economic agent observes a higher selling price than he anticipated. He takes this price rise to be in some part a temporary increase in his relative price or real rate of return and so raises his output. He does so because the substitutability of leisure overtime is high so that a small change in the return on the current work effort can induce a large change in the same direction in the amount of work done. The basic equilibrium model also combines workers and firms into a single worker-entrepreneur group that supplies more (less) of both labor and output when faced with unanticipated rise (fall) in selling prices.[10]

These reactions on the part of the economic agent cannot but lead to forecasting errors that can be recognized with the passage of time as outside price data become available. By then it is, of course, too late to make changes and correct erroneous decisions made. But such long and varied information lags implied in the basic equilibrium model of cycles are even less likely under rational than under adaptive expectations. Critics have underscored that the type of informational problems suggested by the basic equilibrium model can be only very short-term and associated with random changes and not persistent cyclical fluctuations in output and employment.[11] Moreover, temporary misperceptions of monetary and price changes, in the view of critics, would be detected and corrected before they could give rise to large cumulative movements in either direction.[12]

Other critics zero in on the model's assumption of continuous equilibrium in the labor market. It is during recessions and depressions that involuntary layoffs and separations account for the bulk of the unemployed. Fewer people quit jobs during periods when vacancies decline. During such periods more people are looking for work at current or lower wages over longer average time periods.[13]

NOTES

1. The many studies available are simply too numerous to list here. For those of relatively recent vintage, see for instance, Victor Zarnowitz, "Recent Work in Business Cycles in Historical Perspective," *Journal of Economic Literature*, June 1985, pp. 523–80; Robert J. Barro, ed., *Money Expectations and Business Cycles* (New York: Academic Press, 1981); Paul Wachtel, *Crises in the Economic and Financial Structure* (Lexington, Mass.: Lexington Books, 1982); Martin Bronfenbrenner, ed., *Is the Business Cycle Obsolete?* (New York: John Wiley, 1969); Phillip Cagan, *Determinants and Effects of Changes in the Stock of Money 1875–1960* (New York: Columbia University Press for NBER, 1965); Milton Friedman and Anna J. Schwartz, *A Monetary History of the United States, 1867–1960* (Washington, D.C.: National Bureau of Economic Research, 1963); James H. Gapinski, *Macroeconomic Theory: Statics, Dynamics and Policy* (New York: McGraw-Hill, 1980); Robert J. Gordon, "Output Fluctuations and

Gradual Price Adjustment," *Journal of Economic Literature*, June 1981, pp. 493–530.

2. Robert E. Lucas, Jr., "An Equilibrium Model of the Business Cycle," *Journal of Political Economy*, December 1975, pp. 1133–44; Robert E. Lucas, Jr., "Understanding Business Cycles," in *Stabilization of the Domestic and International Economy*, ed. Karl Brunner and Allan H. Meltzer, Carnegie-Rochester Conference Series, Vol. 5 (Amsterdam: North Holland, 1977) pp. 7–30. See also Zarnovitz, "Recent Work in Business Cycles in Historical Perspective," and Kevin D. Hoover, "Two Types of Monetarism," *Journal of Economic Literature*, March 1984, pp. 58–76, for a succinct discussion of a number of these points.

3. See Robert E. Lucas, Jr. and Thomas J. Sargent, eds. *Rational Expectations and Econometric Practice* (Minneapolis: University of Minnesota Press, 1981).

4. Indeed Zarnovitz writes that in the rational expectations models (RE)

the ruling research strategy . . . is to demonstrate for each particular model that one or more of the selected factors can contribute to fluctuations in total output or employment, while recognizing that others can do so as well. The authors are mainly concerned with theoretical possibilities rather than explanations of what actually happens. There is in general little regard for how the pieces fit each other or the "real world." The variety of models is only loosely limited by the ingenuity of the theorists, but many offered hypotheses are not tested and some are not testable. Small linear models are favored because of their mathematical tractability in the equilibrium and RE framework, but this certainly does not mean that larger and/or nonlinear systems are somehow inferior. The criterion of conformity to stylized facts would, in fact, suggest the opposite.

"Recent Work in Business Cycles in Historical Perspective," p. 570.

5. Friedman and Schwartz, *A Monetary History of the United States, 1870–1960*, and *Monetary Trends in the United States and the United Kingdom: Their Relation to Income, Prices and Interest Rates, 1867–1975*. (Chicago: University of Chicago Press, 1982).

6. Adam Smith, *An Inquiry into the Nature and Causes of the Wealth of Nations*. Reprinted edition (Chicago: University of Chicago Press, 1976).

7. George Macesich, "Sources of Monetary Disturbances in the United States, 1834–45," *Journal of Economic History*, September 1960; George Macesich, *The International Monetary Economy and the Third World* (New York: Praeger, 1981); George Macesich, *The*

Politics of Monetarism: Its Historical and Institutional Development (Totowa, N.J.: Rowman and Allanheld, 1984).

8. F. A. Hayek, *Monetary Theory and the Trade Cycle* (New York: Harcourt Brace and Company, 1933); F. A. Hayek, *Profits, Interest and Investment* (London: George Routledge and Sons, 1939).

9. See, for example, Zarnovitz, "Recent Work in Business Cycles in Historical Perspective," p. 552.

10. For a detailed discussion of these and related issues, see *ibid.*

11. See, for instance, F. Modigliani, "The Monetarist Controversy or, Should We Foresake Stabilization Policies?" *American Economic Review* March 1977, pp. 1–19; James Tobin, "How Dead Is Keynes?" *Economic Inquiry* October 1977, pp. 459–68.

12. Zarnowitz, "Recent Work in Business Cycles in Historical Perspective," p. 554.

13. A. M. Okun, "Rational-Expectations-with-Misperceptions as a Theory of Business Cycles," *Journal of Money, Credit and Banking*, November 1980, pp. 817–25.

CHAPTER 7

A Look at the Evidence

As useful as general criticism is of the new classicals and their general equilibrium model, it is not as persuasive as testing the model's implication against available empirical evidence.

A number of studies have in fact tested one or another of the model's implications.[1] These include Barro's estimation of the monetary authorities by regressing the rate of growth in money on its own past values and selected lagged variables and identifying the residuals from this regression with the unanticipated component of monetary change. As Zarnowitz notes,

these tests could not reject the joint hypothesis of rationality and neutrality of money, but many doubts were raised about the specification and identifiability of Barro's reaction function as well as its consistency with private and public rational behavior . . . it is primarily responsible for Mishkin's conclusions being the opposite of that reached in the Barro papers, where lags of two years or ten quarters are used. No attempts to rationalize the persistence of such long distributed lags under REH are made in any of these reports.[2]

In effect, Mishkin's study rejects the neutrality hypothesis that anticipated money growth has no real effects. To judge from his reported results, anticipated as well as unanticipated money growth influence output and unemployment with lags up to 20 quarters.

Other studies cast doubt on new classical models in which prices are fully flexible, and show that output is in fact positively associated with these measured and knowable values of the money stock.[3] Similar dissappointment is registered in subsequent testing of the labor supply function postulated by the new classical studies. In effect, these studies suggest less than satisfactory performance of the new classical models, prompting some adherents of these models to conclude that perhaps the equilibrium approach to business cycles and flexible price equilibrium models leaves something to be desired.

In order to better illustrate the problems at hand I draw upon a study by Munir A. S. Choudhary and myself.[4] The specific issue we examine is whether in fact only the unanticipated component of the money supply growth can effect real output and whether the impact of the unanticipated money supply growth on real output is inversely related to its variance. The experience of 50 countries is drawn upon.

One of the major problems in testing the above hypothesis involves the decomposition of money growth into anticipated and unanticipated components. In the 50-country sample the money supply growth is decomposed on the assumption that monetary authorities are primarily engaged in controlling such macro variables as inflation, real output, and growth. The cross-country tests presented are inconsistent with the hypothesis that only the unanticipated money supply growth can effect real output. Indeed, these results are consistent with those discussed above.

A key hypothesis in the new classical model consists of two propositions: (1) the short-run Phillips curve exists only if aggregate demand is unanticipated; (2) the slope of the short-run Phillips curve is inversely related to the variance of unanticipated aggregate demand. Proposition 1 has been tested extensively for the United States using annual or quarterly data.[5] A critical issue in testing proposition 1 involves the decomposition of aggregate demand into anticipated and unanticipated components.[6] If a relevant variable is omitted in the decomposition of aggregate demand into anticipated and unanticipated components, the decomposition of aggregate demand will be misleading as will the empirical evidence. Thus it is, for example, that Barro and Rush found strong support for proposition 1 using U.S. postwar quarterly data.[7] On the other hand, Merrick found strong rejection of proposition 1 using the same data series, but a different procedure for decomposing the growth into anticipated and unanticipated components.[8] The empirical controversy over proposition 1 remains to be settled.

The validity of proposition 1 is implicitly accepted in proposition 2 as a strong proposition of the new classical model's macro rational expectation hypothesis. In Lucas's equilibrium model of the business cycle, an unanticipated change in aggregate demand influences real output for the reason that it is misperceived as a change in relative demand.[9] If unanticipated aggregate demand is very volatile, the proportion of unanticipated change in aggregate demand, which will be misperceived as relative demand change, will be lower, compared to the situation in which unanticipated aggregate demand is less volatile. Thus acceptance of proposition 2 means also acceptance of proposition 1.

Lucas was the first to test the macro rational expectation hypothesis (MREH) in the form of proposition 2.[10] He regressed the real income on the changes in nominal income for each of 18 countries in the sample, and found that regression coefficients measuring the effect of change in nominal income on real output were lower for two countries (Argentina and Paraguay) compared to the other 16 countries in the sample, and the variance of nominal income was greatest for these two countries. In effect, the study provides support for proposition 2.

Alberro extended the Lucas study to a sample of 50 countries with results consistent with those reported on by Lucas for proposition 2.[11] Kormendi and Meguire demonstrated that cross-country evidence produced by the Lucas-type studies is also in accordance with the prediction of policy-invariant Phillips curve models.[12] Following Kormendi and Meguire it can further be stated that the empirical evidence produced by a Lucas-type study does not necessarily support proposition 2.

Let us suppose, for instance, that variance of unanticipated money growth is the same for two countries, then regardless of the variance of money growth in the two countries, proposition 2 will hold only if the impact of money growth is the same for the two countries. In the above situation, if the variance of money growth differs across the countries, the Lucas-type test will reject proposition 2 when in fact it is true, and vice-versa. Proposition 2 states that impact of unanticipated change in aggregate demand on real output is inversely related to its variance; thus, the more appropriate test will be to investigate the relationship between the variance of unanticipated change in aggregate demand and its effects on real output across the countries. Kormendi and Meguire investigated the relationship between the variance of monetary shocks and the impact of these monetary shocks on the real output of 47 countries. They found strong support for proposition 2. Attfield and Duck also found strong support for proposition 2 by comparing the impact of monetary shocks and the variance of monetary shocks for 11 countries.[13]

As noted above, satisfactory decomposition of aggregate demand into anticipated and unanticipated components is crucial for the validity of empirical tests of the macro rational expectation hypothesis. The procedure used by Kormendi and Meguire in decomposing the money growth into anticipated and unanticipated components does not significantly differentiate their work from that of Lucas. In their study, for 27 out of 47 countries unanticipated money growth is equal to money growth.

CROSS-COUNTRY TESTS WITH MISSPECIFICATION OF THE MONEY SUPPLY EQUATION

For reasons already discussed, the satisfactory decomposition of aggregate demand shock into anticipated and unanticipated components is crucial in testing proposition 1 of MREH. This problem of decomposition becomes even more crucial when proposition 2 of MREH is tested across the countries. For example, let us suppose that the true money supply process for countries A and B is given by equations 1 and 2. Furthermore, it is assumed that the money supply process is known to the public in their respective countries, and their expectations are rational in the sense of Muth.

$$M_t = ao + a1X_{1t} + a2X_{2t} + e_t \tag{1}$$

$$M_t = ao + a1X_{1t} + c_t \qquad c_t \; (o, \sigma^2) \tag{2}$$

M_t is money supply; X_{1t}, X_{2t} are the goal variables; e_t is random error with zero mean and constant variance. According to proposition 2 of MREH, the effect of monetary shocks will be the same for both countries. Now suppose that equation 2 is used to decompose the money across both countries. The computed variance for unanticipated money supply (VRM) for countries A and B is the following:

$$VRM(A) - (a2)^2 \, var(X_{2t}) + \sigma^2 \tag{3}$$

$$VRM(B) = \sigma^2 \tag{4}$$

If $var(X_{2t}) \neq 0$, then the computed variance for country A will be larger than that for country B. Thus, empirical studies with cross-country misspecification of the money supply equation will reject proposition 2 of MREH when, in fact, the proposition holds, and vice versa.

SPECIFICATION ISSUE

Money Supply Equation

There is no statistical test that can be used to check whether or not the decomposition of money growth into anticipated and unanticipated components was correct. The problem of decomposing the money supply must be settled on theoretical grounds. A precise decomposition is an impossible task because we simply do not know what type of monetary policy was followed in each country, or the amount of information (quantitative or qualitative) available to the public to predict the monetary policy. If the best is not available, the second best is always preferred. It is well-known that since World War II, monetary authorities have been actively engaged (wrongly or rightly) in controlling such macroeconomic variables as real output growth rate, inflation rate, interest rates, and so on, in almost every country of the world. Information on some of these macroeconomic variables (growth rate of real output, inflation rate) is also readily available to the public in almost all countries. On the assumption that monetary authorities were actively engaged in controlling the real output growth or inflation rate or both across the countries, the following money supply equation is specified to decompose the money growth rate into anticipated and unanticipated components.

$$M_t = a0 + a1(L)M_t = a2(L)P_t + a3(L)Y_t = a4T + RM_t \tag{5}$$

The variables M_t, P_t, Y_t are the first difference of the natural logs of money supply, consumer price, and real output, respectively. T is the time trend variable. RM_t is random error indistinguishable from white noise. L is the polynomial in the lag operator, for example

$$a1(L)M_t = \sum_{i=1}^{n} a1iM_{t-1} \tag{6}$$

Only P and Y variables are selected among the other macroeconomic variables for the money supply equation because we believe that monetary authorities were mainly engaged in controlling the behavior of these variables; furthermore, information on these variables was readily available to the public to predict the stance of monetary policy.

Given the general specification of money supply equation (5), the following procedure was used to select the variate of equation (5) for each country in the sample. First, the appropriate lag length of M in the autoregression model is selected using Theil's minimum standard criteria. The lag length that yields minimum standard error (highest adjusted rate R-square [$\bar{R}^2$]) is selected. If the $\bar{R}^2$ at selected lags is negative, the variable is deleted from the money supply equation. Thus, the first step requires estimation of the money supply equation in the following form, with varying lag length of M from 1 to n.

$$M_t = a0 = al(L)M_t + e_t \tag{7}$$

Once the appropriate lag length for M is selected, the money supply equation is estimated in the bivariate form as given below to select the appropriate lag length for other variables, by keeping the selected lags of M (if any) and varying the lag length of the second variable from 1 to n.

$$M_t = a1 + \sum_{i=1}^{k} ali\ M_{t-1} = aj(L)X_t \tag{8}$$

$$J = 2,3,4$$
$$k \leq n.$$

K is the maximum lag length selected for M in the autoregression model. X_t represents the second variable in the equation (P, Y, T). In the bivariate specification, the maximum lag length for the P or Y or T variable is selected, using the maximum $\bar{R}^2$ criteria. The second variable that produces the highest $\bar{R}^2$ in the bivariate model is retained with its selected lags. Once the second variable is selected (if any) with its appropriate lags, trivariate specification is used to select the third variable with its appropriate lags, by keeping the selected lags of M and of the second variable (X) and varying the lags of the third variable from 1 to m. This requires estimation of the following form: M is the lag selected for the variable in the bivariate model;

$$M_t = a0 + \sum_{i=1}^{k} aliM_{t-1} + \sum_{i=1}^{L} ajiX_{t-1} + ap(L)Z_t \tag{9}$$

$$P \neq j;\ P = 2,3,4;\ L \leq n$$

L is the maximum lag length selected for X_t in the bivariate model; Z_t is the variable not selected in the bivariate model. The third variable that increases the $\bar{R}^2$ most is retained with its selected lags. Once the third variable is selected (if any) the process is repeated for the selection of the fourth variable with its appropriate lags. It should be noted that in each step the new variable is retained if its inclusion increases the $\bar{R}^2$. The maximum lag length is predetermined to be 4 for each variable (n = 4).

Real Output Equation

The specification for the real output equation used here is similar to one used by Barro (1978) in the sense that only the unanticipated money supply matters for real output.[14] The specification for the real output equation is given below:

$$Y_t = CO + \sum_{i=1}^{4} BiRM_{t=i} + \Lambda T + U_t \tag{10}$$

U_t is random error indistinguishable from white noise. The trend variable (T) is retained in the output equation if its inclusion increases $\bar{R}^2$.

EMPIRICAL RESULTS

The Data

Data for all countries are from international financial statistics yearbooks and international financial statistics.[15] Y is real gross domestic product (GDP) or real gross national product in 1980 prices. Where data on real GDP or real GNP are not available, the GDP or GNP in current prices is deflated by the consumer price index. P is the consumer price index, with 1980 as the base year. M is the money supply (M1 definition).

The data consist of annual observations from 1955 to the most recent available observation on all three variables (M, Y, P). The data selected are from 1955 onward, because the series available before 1955 are not coparable for one or more variables, owing to substantial revision in the data. The data for M, P, and Y series were logged and differenced, and showed no evidence of being nonstationary.

Examination of Residuals

Once a model has been specified and its parameters estimated, a check must be made to see whether or not the model specification was correct. If the residuals for each equation in the model are not autocorrelated, then the model is correctly specified. Unfortunately, there is no general agreement over the choice of a test that can be used to detect autocorrelation in residuals. The Box-Pierce Q-statistic is one of the tests widely used to detect autocorrelation residuals.[16] The Box-Pierce test (Q-test) is a cumulative autocorrelation test and is approximately distributed as chi-square. For safety, besides the Q-test, we have also used the Durbin F-test to detect autocorrelation in residuals.[17] The Durbin F-test is the cumulative equivalent of the Durbin h-test. The Durbin F-test is performed as given below:

$$e_t - cO = C1(L)e_t + C2\,X_t + Re_t \qquad (11)$$

e_t is the residual obtained from the original specification of the equation; X_t is the independent variable in the original specification; L is the polynomial lag operator; Re_t is the random error term. If the null hypothesis that each $Cli = 0$, $i = 1 \ldots n$ is accepted, then the model specification is accepted.

In Tables 1, 2 and 3 of our study, which are reproduced in the Appendix to this chapter, estimates of the money supply equation and of the real output equation are presented using the procedure given in the section entitled "Specification Issue." The Box-Pierce Q-test and the Durbin F-test are also presented in these tables to test the specification for the money supply and real output equations, respectively. The following criteria were used to check the specification of each equation: If the null hypothesis of no autocorrelation is rejected by both tests at the 10 percent level or by either test at the 5 percent level, then misspecification of the equation is accepted. In case autocorrelation is detected using the criteria given above, the Cochrane-Orcutt technique is used to correct the autocorrelation in residuals.

Preliminary test results showed that the specification for

the money supply equation given in the "Specification Issue" section was accepted for 49 out of 50 countries in the sample. The only country for which the specification of the money supply equation was rejected is Ghana. Test results reported for Ghana in Table 1 are after the second-order autocorrelation in residuals was corrected using the Cochrane-Orcutt procedure. The specification for output equation was accepted for all but four countries (El Salvador, Nigeria, Sweden, Trinidad and Tobago). The estimates reported for these countries in Table 2 are after the second order autocorrelation in residuals was corrected using the Cochrane-Orcutt technique.

THE CROSS-COUNTRY EVIDENCE

With Imposing The Long-Run Neutrality Constraint

Our results in Figure 1 in the Appendix suggest the relationship between the peak effect of monetary shocks (X_2) and the variance of these monetary shocks (VRM) across 50 countries. X_2 represents the maximum effect of monetary shocks over up to two lag periods, with imposing the restriction that the effect of monetary shocks disappears over the four-lag period. The examination of the relationship between the peak effect of monetary shocks and its variance, across the countries in the sample, does not show even weak support for proposition 2 of MREH. As shown in our test results, the country with the highest variance of monetary shocks (Nigeria) has the third highest peak effect of monetary shocks; and the country with the second highest variance of aggregate demand shocks (Bolivia) has the second lowest peak effect of monetary shocks. Similarly, countries with the lowest variance of aggregate demand are not necessarily the countries where peak effect is highest. For example, the United States has the lowest variance of monetary shocks and the highest peak effect of monetary shocks; and Norway, with the second lowest variance of monetary shocks, has the lowest peak effect of monetary shocks. Similar evidence holds for other countries that fall between these two extreme ranges of the variance of aggregate demand shocks. That is, countries with a larger variance of monetary shocks are not necessarily the countries with lower peak effects of monetary shocks.

Without Imposing the Long-Run Neutrality Constraint

Our study also examines in Figure 2 the peak effect of monetary shocks (X_1) and the variance of monetary shocks across 50 countries, without imposing the restriction that neutrality occurs over four lags. X_1 is measured as the maximum effect of monetary shocks up to a four-lag period. The results in Figure 2 show that rejection of proposition 2 of MREH is even stronger when long-run neutrality is not imposed. The countries with the highest variance of monetary shocks are definitely not those where the peak effect of monetary shocks is lowest. The evidence in Figure 2 suggests a positive relationship between the variance of monetary shocks and the impact of monetary shocks across the countries, rather than the negative relationship predicted by MREH.

A MORE RATIONAL VIEW?

The evidence discussed suggests that empirical support for proposition 2 of MREH is weak in our cross-country study of 50 countries. We believe that the evidence, such as it is, appears more consistent in accordance with views presented by Friedman and other monetarists.[18] Monetarist models, as we have discussed, differ from MREH regarding the speed of adjustments in the habits and attitude of the public, as well as in financial and other institutional arrangements, to changes in the monetary system. According to proponents of MREH, these adjustments are instantaneous; to monetarists, however, these changes occur slowly over time. For example, regarding the transitional period over which complete adjustment will occur, Friedman states: "Such a transitional period may well extend over decades."[19] Thus, in the monetarist model, monetary changes (anticipated or unanticipated) will affect real output in the transitional period unless the monetary policy is steady for decades. As Macesich and Tsai point out, a country's economic, legal, political, and social systems do influence the role money can play.[20] In countries whose economic, legal, political, and social systems are favorable to the adjustment process, the peak effect of monetary shocks will be lower, compared to the countries where these factors are unfavorable to the adjustment process, regardless of the variance of monetary shocks.

The empirical evidence cited and discussed in this study about the data in the Appendix is supportive of this hypothesis. There are many countries in our sample in which the variance of monetary shocks is almost the same, but the peak effect of monetary shocks varies substantially across these countries. For example, the variance of monetary shocks is almost the same for the United States and Norway, but the difference in the peak effect of monetary shocks is larger for these two countries than for any other pair of countries in the sample. Similarly, there are many countries where the peak effect of monetary shocks is identical, but where there is a substantial difference in the variance of monetary shocks. It could well be that difference in the sociopolitical economic and legal systems in the several countries cloud over the predicted results of MREH. A useful extension of this study would be to explicitly model the effect of these various country systems.

CONCLUSION

Most of the empirical studies directed at testing MREH have investigated proposition 1, especially for the United States. Only a few empirical studies have investigated proposition 2, and almost all of them found support for MREH. As Kormendi and Meguire pointed out, however, empirical support for MREH using a Lucas-type test procedure is indeed invalid. The correct procedure to test proposition 2 of MREH is to compare the impact of monetary shocks and their variance across countries. Only two studies appear to have adopted this procedure (Kormendi and Meguire; Attfield and Duck). Both studies provide strong empirical support for proposition 2. The empirical evidence provided by Kormendi and Meguire is questionable on the grounds that their decomposition of the money growth rate into anticipated and unanticipated components is not in accordance with the rational expectations hypothesis. According to that hypothesis, the public uses all available relevant information to predict the behavior of monetary policy. In this study we have used a procedure for decomposing the money growth into anticipated and unanticipated components, which is more in accordance with the rational expectations hypothesis, and thus provides a better test of MREH across countries. For example, according to Kormendi and Meguire, the money growth process is completely unpredictable for Israel; however, our study shows that more than 90 percent of the money growth was predictable on the basis of available information. Our study does not show even weak support for proposition 2 of MREH.

Although the decomposition of money growth is more satisfactory in the Attfield and Duck study than in that of Kormendi and Meguire, their cross-country sample is too small to generalize the evidence. For example, our study suggests that a different subsample can be used to strongly support or reject the MREH.

For reasons already noted, caution should be the guideline in judging the empirical results and tests of the MREH in this and other studies. Most studies including this one may be subject to the same criticism we have used to reject the Kormendi and Meguire study. For example, a more reliable decomposition requires a detailed study of all the relevant factors determining the money supply in each individual country. The money supply function, in particular, may not be stable over time. It is, moreover, an open question whether in fact we can specify money as a function of the same basic variables across countries.[21] It may well be that a country-by-country analysis would provide a more fruitful approach to testing the MREH hypothesis. Given their limitations, these cross-country results do suggest reasons for the less than enthusiastic support that many economists, including Friedman and kindred monetarists, have given MREH.

NOTES

1. See, for instance, the discussion of a number of these attempts in Victor Zarnowitz, "Recent work in Business Cycles in Historical Perspective," *Journal of Economic Literature*, June 1985, pp. 523–80. Robert E. Lucas, Jr., "Some International Evidence on Output-Inflation Tradeoffs," *American Economic Review*, June 1973, pp. 326–34; Robert E. Lucas, Jr., "An Equilibrium Model of the Business Cycle," *Journal of Political Economy*, December 1975, pp. 1113–44; F. S. Mishkin, "Does Anticipated Monetary Policy Matter? An Econometric Investigation," *Journal of Political Economy*, February 1982, pp. 22–51; R. J. Barro, "Unanticipated Money Growth and Unemployment in the United States," *American Economic Review*, March 1977, pp. 101–15; R. J. Barro and Mark Rush, "Unanticipated Money and Economic Activity," in *Rational Expectations and Economic Policy*, ed. by Stanley Fischer, A Conference Report (Chicago: University of Chicago Press, 1980), pp. 23–48 and discussion pp. 40–75; Roger C. Kormendi and Philip G. Meguire, "Cross-Regime Evidence of Macroeconomic Rationality," *Journal of Political Economy*, November 1984, pp. 875–908.

2. Zarnowitz, "Recent Work in Business Cycles in Historical Perspective," p. 554.

3. REH is an abbreviation for "rational expectations hypothesis." See, for instance, J. F. Boschen and H. I. Grossman, "Test of Equilibrium Macroeconomics Using Contemporaneous Monetary Data," *Journal of Monetary Economics*, November 1982, pp. 309–33; B. T. McCallum, "Macroeconomics After A Decade of Rational Expectations: Some Critical Issues," *Federal Reserve Bank of Richmond Economic Review*, December 1982, pp. 3–12.

4. The results reported in this chapter draw upon George Macesich and Munir A. S. Choudhary, "Cross-Country Tests of the Macro-Rational Expectations Hypothesis" (unpublished manuscript).

5. See, for instance, Barro, "Unanticipated Money Growth and Unemployment in the United States," pp. 101–15; R. J. Barro, "Unanticipated Money, Output, and Price Level in the United States," *Journal of Political Economy*, August 1978, pp. 549–80; Barro and Rush, "Unanticipated Money and Economic Activity"; Robert J. Gordon, "Price Inertia and Policy Ineffectiveness in the United States, 1960–80," *Journal of Political Economy*, December 1982, pp. 1087–117; F. S. Mishkin, "Does Anticipated Monetary Policy Matter?" pp. 22–51.

6. For a model that does not require decomposition of aggregate demand, see Robert T. McGee and Richard T. Stasiak, "Does Antici-

pated Monetary Policy Matter? Another Look," *Journal of Money, Credit and Banking*, February 1985, pp. 16–27.

7. Barro and Rush, "Unanticipated Money and Economic Activity."

8. J. J. Merrick, Jr., "Financial Market Efficiency, the Decomposition of 'Anticipated' versus 'Unanticipated' Money Growth, and Further Tests of the Relation Between Money and Real Output," *Journal of Money, Credit and Banking*, May 1983, Vol. 15. pp. 222–32.

9. Robert Lucas, Jr., "Understanding Business Cycles," in *Stabilization of the Domestic and International Economy*, ed. by K. Brunner and A. H. Meltzer, Carnegie-Rochester Conference Series, Vol. 5 (Amsterdam: North Holland, 1977), pp. 7–30.

10. Lucas, "Some International Evidence on Output-Inflation Tradeoffs," pp. 326–33.

11. Jose Alberro, "The Lucas Hypothesis in the Phillips Curve: Further International Evidence," *Journal of Monetary Economics*, March 1981, pp. 239–50.

12. Kormendi and Meguire, "Cross-Regime Evidence of Macroeconomic Rationality."

13. C. Attfield and N. Duck, "The Influence of Unanticipated Money Growth on Real Output: Some Cross-Country Estimates," *Journal of Money, Credit and Banking*, November 1983, pp. 442–54.

14. Barro, "Unanticipated Money, Output, and Price Level in the United States."

15. *International Financial Statistical Year Book* (Washington: International Monetary Fund, 1983, 1984, and 1985).

16. G. Box and D. Pierce, "Distribution of Residual Auto-Correlations in Auto-regressive Integrated Moving Average Time-series Models," *Journal of American Statistical Association*, 65, 1970, 1509–26.

17. J. Durbin, "Testing for Social Correlation in Least Squares when the Regressers are Logged Dependent Variables," *Econometrica* 38, 1970, pp. 410–421.

18. Milton Friedman, "Nobel Lecture: Inflation and Unemployment," *Journal of Political Economy* 85, June 1977, pp. 451–472.

19. Friedman, *Ibid.*

20. G. Macesich and H. L. Tsai, *Money in Economic Systems* (New York: Praeger, 1982).

21. Kormendi and Meguire, "Cross-Regime Evidence of Macroeconomic Rationality"; and Attfield and Duck, "The Influence of Unanticipated Money Growth on Real Output."

APPENDIX

Table 1
Specification for Money Supply Equation

Country	Specification for money supply equation					VRM	R^2	$\bar{R}^2$	Q-test	F-test
Australia (1960–83)	M = -.08 (.93)	-.04M-1 (.18)	-.38M-2 (1.33)	+.11M-3 (.33)	-.09M-4 (.30)	.00174	.59	.33	2.37	.02 (13,6)
	-.52X-1 (.77)	+.56Y-2 (.96)	-.20Y-3 (.38)	+1.53Y-4 (2.75)	+.01T (1.43)					
Austria (1960–83)	M = -.05 (1.01)	-.51M-1 (2.25)	+.62P-1 (1.11)	+.72Y-1 (1.24)	-.68Y-2 (1.16)	.00186	.40	.18	2.97	1.42 (4,9)
	+.90Y-3 (1.60)	+.87Y-4 (1.38)								
Belgium (1957–83)	M = -.006 (.31)	+.16M-1 (.88)	+.60P-1 (2.45)	+.79Y-1 (2.41)		.00123	.32	.23	4.30	.39 (4,15)
Bolivia (1959–83)	M = .25 (1.40)	+.53M-1 (1.35)	-.14M-2 (.24)	-.62M-3 (2.19)	-.53P-1 (1.07)	.02185	.73	.60	7.01	1.32 (4,8)
	+1.05P-2 (2.13)	-2.67Y-1 (2.07)	-1.72Y-2 (1.26)	+.01T (1.60)						
Burma (1960–83)	M = -.03 (.54)	+.32M-1 (1.59)	-.09M-2 (.49)	+.130M-3 (.79)	-1.09Y-1 (2.52)	.00497	.63	.43	11.5	1.76 (4,7)
	-.54Y-2 (1.25)	+1.00Y-3 (2.40)	+1.27Y-4 (3.05)	+.004T (1.35)						
Canada (1958–83)	M = -.0006 (.01)	+.44Y-1 (.60)	+1.44Y-2 (1.56)			.00775	.12	.05	7.56	1.36 (4,15)

Table 1—Continued

Country	Specification for money supply equation	VRM	R^2	$\overline{R}^2$	Q-test	F-test
Colombia (1960–83)	M = .14 +.38M-1 -.63M-2 +.35M-3 -.19M-4 (1.98) (1.48) (2.97) (1.26) (.87) +.19P-1 -.16P-2 +.37P-3 -.26P-4 +.003T (1.32) (1.02) (2.75) (1.82) (1.29)	.00075	.73	.55	4.69	3.38* (4,6)
Denmark (1960–83)	M = .11 -.74M-1 -.64M-2 +1.45P-1 +.62P-2 (2.08) (3.09) (2.58) (3.05) (1.02) +.14P-3 -.69P-4 +.89Y-1 (.24) (1.77) (1.56)	.00098	.65	.50	2.20	.56 (4,8)
Dominican Republic (1958–82)	M = -.01 -.45M-1 +.84Y-1 +.57Y-2 +.004T (.24) (.24) (2.29) (2.22) (1.39) (1.38)	.00856	.38	.25	5.68	1.20 (4,12)
Ecuador (1960–83)	M = .04 -.20M-1 +.02M-2 +.38M-3 +.25M-4 (1.08) (1.01) (.10) (2.30) (1.37) +.96Y-1 (2.66)	.00406	.50	.36	8.4	.31 (4,10)
Egypt (1958–83)	M = -.02 +.23M-1 -.14M-2 +.01Y-1 +.49Y-2 (.76) (1.02) (.68) (.02) (1.50) +.01T (2.48)	.00328	.61	.51	9.53	.84 (4,12)
El Salvador (1959–83)	M = -.02 +.09M-1 -.16M-2 +.15M-3 +1.0P-1 (.52) (.49) (.70) (.63) (1.94) +1.1Y-1 (2.58)	.00527	.44	.30	4.16	.63 (4,11)

Table 1—Continued

Country	Specification for money supply equation	VRM	R^2	$\bar{R}^2$	Q-test	F-test
Finland (1960–83)	M = .06 +.48P-1 -.73P-2 -1.00P-3 +.68P-4 (1.41)(.84)(1.09)(1.54)(1.29) +.01T (1.69)	.00435	.35	.17	4.81	.32 (4,10)
France (1960–83)	M = -.03 .22M-1 +.89P-1 +1.55Y-1 +.49Y-2 (.46)(1.09)(2.16)(2.62)(.95) +.15Y-3 -1.01Y-4 (.30)(2.02)	.00094	.42	.22	6.27	.52 (4,9)
Germany (1956–83)	M = .01 -.13T (6.36)(1.41)	.00157	.07	.04	8.18	.75 (4,18)
Ghana (1959–83)	M = -.09 -.28M-1 -.09M-2 +.23M-3 +.02T (.64)(1.24)(.39)(.95)(1.97)	.01692	.43	.30	5.25	3.31* (4,10)
Greece (1958–83)	M = .13 +.05M-1 -.03M-2 +.23P-1 (3.10)(.24)(.15)(1.73)	.00146	.19	.08	2.86	.20 (4,14)
Guatemala (1960–82)	M = .03 +.54M-1 +.26M-2 +.10M-3 -.28P-1 (1.32)(2.59)(1.13)(.44)(.57) +.25P-2 +.86P-3 -1.38P-4 (.36)(1.45)(3.02)	.00240	.66	.49	4.73	.07 (4,7)
Haiti (1959–83)	M = .08 -.16M-1 +.40M-2 +.42M-3 -.64P-1 (2.12)(.83)(1.90)(2.02)(1.38)	.01214	.25	.10	1.87	.26 (4,12)
Honduras (1959–83)	M = .11 +.15M-1 -.02M-2 +.53M-3 -.30Y-1 (2.96)(.68)(.09)(2.61)(.61) -.61Y-2 -.58Y-3 (1.08)(1.13)	.00317	.35	.137	6.35	1.11 (4,10)
Iceland (1960–83)	M = -.03 +.01M-1 -.24M-2 +.26M-3 +.15M-4 (.52)(.05)(1.05)(1.06)(.62) +.01T (2.03)	.00928	.62	.52	3.11	.28 (4,10)

Table 1—Continued

Country	Specification for money supply equation	VRM	R^2	$\bar{R}^2$	Q-test	F-test
India (1960–82)	M = -.05 (.85) +.25M-1 (1.11) -.02M-2 (.07) -.44P-1 (1.74) +.94P-2 (3.19) -.31P-3 (.90) -.25P-4 (.75) +.39Y-1 (1.13) +.26Y-2 (.67) -.06Y-3 (.16) +.43Y-4 (1.30)	.00092	.77	.58	4.39	.42 (4,4)
Ireland (1959–82)	M = .06 (2.32) +.32M-1 (1.62) +.81P-1 (2.05) +1.28Y-1 (2.12) -1.86Y-2 (3.50) +.73Y-3 (1.36) -.004T (1.27)	.00150	.56	.41	2.98	.89 (4,9)
Israel (1960–83)	M = .12 (1.20) +.64M-1 (1.85) -.38M-2 (1.38) -.61M-3 (2.22) -.86M-4 (2.07) +.96P-1 (2.93) +.32P-2 (.73) +1.16P-3 (2.66) +.39Y-1 (.54) +.79Y-2 (1.09) +1.58Y-3 (1.89)	.00419	.92	.85	3.34	.03 (4,5)
Italy (1958–83)	M = .10 (3.74) +.32M-1 (1.83) -.57P-1 (1.91) +.63P-2 (2.09)	.00144	.25	.14	5.72	.45 (4,14)
Jamaica (1959–83)	M = .05 (.98) -.29M-1 (1.31) +.19M-2 (.83) +.16M-3 (.72) +.005T (1.33)	.00700	.26	.11	3.40	.07 (4,12)
Japan (1958–83)	M = .08 (1.41) +.22M-1 (1.21) +.18M-2 (.99) -.40Y-1 (.97) +.89Y-2 (2.31) -.003T (1.62)	.00221	.55	.44	3.03	.64 (4,12)

109

Table 1—Continued

Country	Specification for money supply equation	VRM	R^2	$\bar{R}^2$	Q-test	F-test
Korea (1960–83)	$M = .07 \quad -.17P_{-1} \quad +.62P_{-2} \quad -.48P_{-3} \quad +.77P_{-4}$ $\quad\quad (.71) \quad (.42) \quad\quad (1.58) \quad\quad (1.32) \quad\quad (2.14)$ $\quad\quad +.56Y_{-1} \quad -.68Y_{-2} \quad +.49Y_{-3} \quad +.64Y_{-4}$ $\quad\quad (1.08) \quad\quad (1.28) \quad\quad (.94) \quad\quad (1.18)$	.00706	.46	.18	2.55	.47 (4,7)
Malaysia (1957–83)	$M = -.01 \quad +.04M_{-1} \quad +.006T$ $\quad\quad (.41) \quad\quad (.19) \quad\quad (2.64)$	.00511	.36	.31	5.78	.43 (4,16)
Mexico (1960–83)	$M = .001 \quad +.002M_{-1} \quad +.0003M_{-2} \quad -.05M_{-3}$ $\quad\quad (.01) \quad\quad (.01) \quad\quad\quad (.001) \quad\quad\quad (.15)$ $\quad\quad +.37M_{-4} \quad -.06P_{-1} \quad +.54P_{-2} \quad +.006T$ $\quad\quad (1.22) \quad\quad (.20) \quad\quad (1.79) \quad\quad (1.65)$	.00202	.82	.74	2.94	.54 (4,18)
Netherlands (1960–83)	$M = .07 \quad +.70P_{-1} \quad -.29P_{-2} \quad +.83P_{-3} \quad -1.1P_{-1}$ $\quad\quad (2.86) \quad (1.20) \quad\quad (.42) \quad\quad (1.44) \quad\quad (2.31)$	.00157	.25	.10	3.21	.12 (4,11)
Nigeria (1959–83)	$M = .08 \quad +.46M_{-1} \quad +.16Y_{-1} \quad -.82Y_{-2} \quad +.70Y_{-3}$ $\quad\quad (1.72) \quad (2.16) \quad\quad (.39) \quad\quad (2.02) \quad\quad (1.77)$	.02193	.32	.18	7.84	.73 (4,12)
New Zealand (1957–82)	$M = .06 \quad +.32M_{-1} \quad +.17P_{-1} \quad -1.01Y_{-1}$ $\quad\quad (2.14) \quad (1.68) \quad\quad (1.25) \quad\quad (1.49)$	.00491	.23	.12	6.89	1.08 (4,14)
Norway (1960–83)	$M = .04 \quad +.14M_{-1} \quad +.20M_{-2} \quad -.21P_{-1} \quad -.18P_{-2}$ $\quad\quad (1.96) \quad (.61) \quad\quad (1.36) \quad\quad (1.92) \quad\quad (1.33)$ $\quad\quad -.42P_{-3} \quad +.19P_{-4} \quad +.003T$ $\quad\quad (3.04) \quad\quad (1.15) \quad\quad (1.65)$	.00060	.69	.56	4.22	.80 (4,8)
Panama (1959–83)	$M = .14 \quad -.22M_{-1} \quad +.17M_{-2} \quad -.22M_{-3} \quad +1.21Y_{-1}$ $\quad\quad (2.02) \quad (1.00) \quad\quad (.77) \quad\quad (1.06) \quad\quad (1.72)$ $\quad\quad -.42Y_{-2} \quad -1.17Y_{-3}$ $\quad\quad (.66) \quad\quad (1.63)$	.00757	.33	.11	3.46	1.68 (4,10)

Table 1—Continued

Country	Specification for money supply equation	VRM	R^2	$\bar{R}^2$	Q-test	F-test
Paraguay (1956–83)	M = RM	.01403	---	---	13.09	.75 (4,19)
Peru (1960–83)	M = .09 (1.81) +.55M-1 (1.83) -.48M-2 (2.63) -.49M-3 (2.80) +.32M-4 (1.51) -.91P-1 (2.65) +1.54P-2 (4.24) -.87P-3 (1.90) +.68P-4 (1.78) -.99Y-1 (2.24) +.01T (1.94)	.00271	.88	.80	5.45	1.39 (4,5)
Philippines (1956–83)	M = .07 (2.32) +.003T (1.97)	.00549	.13	.10	3.74	.33 (4,18)
Portugal (1960–82)	M = .01 (.21) -.07M-1 (.33) +1.18P-1 (2.04) -.09P-2 (.14) -.43P-3 (.77) +.84Y-1 (1.48) +.16Y-2 (.27) +1.04Y-3 (1.84) -1.06Y-4 (2.18)	.00198	.64	.43	5.95	.01 (12,6)
South Africa (1957–83)	M = -.002 (.69) +.35M-1 (1.85) +.005T (2.31)	.00373	.52	.48	8.17	1.25 (4,16)
Spain (1958–83)	M = .10 (3.34) +.39M-1 (1.86) +.25P-1 (.83) -.49P-2 (1.75)	.00177	.32	.23	3.99	1.23 (4,14)
Sri Lanka (1959–83)	M = -.002 (.07) +.21M-1 (.99) -.34M-2 (1.73) +.30M-3 (1.41) +.006T (1.70)	.00381	.48	.37	4.15	.31 (4,12)
Sweden (1957–83)	M = -.04 (2.14) +.62P-1 (2.04)	.00232	.14	.11	4.39	1.08 (4,17)

111

Table 1—Continued

Country	Specification for money supply equation	VRM	R^2	$\bar{R}^2$	Q-test	F-test
Switzerland (1960–83)	M = .09 +.17M-1 +.06M-2 -.83M-3 -.27M-4 (3.28) (.84) (.84) (4.50) (1.19) +.17Y-1 +1.51Y-2 -1.20Y-3 +.81Y-4 (.41) (3.52) (2.57) (2.12)	.00130	.68	.51	6.54	2.89 $(4,7)$
Thailand (1958–83)	M = .04 +.37M-1 -.13M-2 -.43P-1 +.003T (1.34) (1.85) (.53) (1.54) (1.89)	.00260	.34	.22	4.60	.20 $(4,13)$
Trinidad & Tobago (1959–82)	M = .001 -.32M-1 -.27M-2 +.004M-3 +.69P-1 (.04) (1.44) (1.57) (.02) (1.31) +1.23P-2 +1.18P-3 (1.80) (1.58)	.00420	.75	.66	5.42	.64 $(4,9)$
Turkey (1960–83)	M = -.02 +.52M-1 -.28M-2 -.34M-3 -.08P-1 (.60) (1.27) (.67) (1.13) (.41) +.10P-2 -.15P-3 +.28P-4 +.15T (.54) (.89) (1.18) (2.38)	.00160	.87	.80	5.14	1.00 $(4,7)$
United Kingdom (1960–83)	M = .001 -.30M-1 -.37M-2 -.43M-3 +.29M-4 (.03) (1.43) (1.58) (1.93) (1.35) +.52P-1 +1.07P-2 +.42Y-1 +1.07Y-2 -.67Y-3 (1.34) (2.22) (.59) (1.48) (1.18)	.00122	.70	.51	6.31	.94 $(4,6)$
United States (1960–83)	M = .003 +.13M-1 -.46M-2 +.19M-3 +.93M-4 (.18) (.58) (2.27) (.72) (2.55) +.44Y-1 -.43Y-3 (1.89) (2.43)	.000154	.65	.49	5.94	.11 $(4,8)$
Venezuela (1960–83)	M = .01 +.51M-1 -.15M-2 +34M-3 -.39M-4 (.19) (2.47) (.65) (1.61) (2.06) +.005T (1.41)	.00537	.52	.38	4.90	.55 $(4,10)$

112

Source: George Macesich and Munir A. S. Choudhary, "Cross-Country Tests of the Macro-Rational Expectations Hypothesis," unpublished manuscript.

Notes: M, Y, and P represent money supply (M1 definition), real output, and consumer price index, respectively. The variables are logged and differenced. M_{-i}, Y_{-i}, and P_{-i} represent ith lag of the respective variable. T is the time trend variable. The white noise term in the money supply equation is RM. The absolute value of t-statistics is given in parentheses under the estimated regression coefficients. VRM is the variance of (RM). $\bar{R}^2$ is R^2 adjusted for degree of freedom. Q-test is Box-Pierce statistics computed over first 10 RM. F-test is Durbin-F statistics. The values in parentheses under Q-test represent the degree of freedom. Estimates reported for Ghana are after the second-order autocorrelation in residuals was corrected by using Cochrane-Orcutt technique.

* Specification rejected at 10 percent level.
** Specification rejected at 5 percent level.

Table 2
Real Output Equation (Unrestricted Ordinary Least Squares [OLS]:

$$Y = CO + \sum_{i=0}^{4} BiRMt - i + \lambda T + UT$$

Country	B0	B1	B2	B3	B4	λ	X1	F	R^2	$\bar{R}^2$	Q-test	F-test
Australia (1964–83)	-.023 (.27)	.040 (.40)	-.240 (1.57)	-.062 (.36)	-.079 (.54)	-.002 (1.59)	.017	3.46 (6,13)	.61	.44	4.68	.18 (4,5)
Austria (1964–83)	.038 (.45)	.206 (2.15)	.028 (.28)	-.089 (.92)	.119 (1.20)	-.002 (2.48)	.303	2.99 (6,13)	.58	.39	5.54	.44 (4,5)
Belgium (1961–83)	-.067 (.44)	.087 (.56)	-.022 (.14)	-.317 (1.96)	-.137 (.88)	-.002 (1.95)	.020	1.39 (6,16)	.34	.10	4.06	.99 (4,8)
Bolivia (1963–83)	-.071 (1.46)	.011 (.23)	.113 (1.70)	.096 (1.23)	.124 (1.57)	-.004 (3.36)	.273	6.08 (6,14)	.72	.60	6.1	.79 (4,6)
Burma (1964–83)	.034 (.26)	-.318 (2.83)	.298 (2.58)	-.080 (.70)	-.142 (1.29)	.004 (2.69)	.034	3.5 (6,13)	.62	.44	5.65	1.79 (4,5)
Canada (1962–83)	-.086 (1.59)	.004 (.06)	-.070 (1.19)	-.100 (1.70)	.009 (.16)	-.003 (3.94)	-.082	3.70 (6,15)	.60	.44	7.33	1.58 (4,7)
Colombia (1964–83)	.263 (1.81)	.120 (.70)	-.013 (.08)	-.026 (.166)	-.391 (2.36)	-.002 (2.01)	.383	3.24 (6,13)	.61	.41	14.16	.81 (4,5)
Denmark (1964–83)	.197 (1.34)	.254 (1.46)	-.287 (1.73)	.142 (.86)	.220 (1.26)	-.002 (2.11)	.526	3.19 (6,13)	.60	.41	8.00	1.50 (4,5)
Dominican Republic (1962–83)	.135 (1.08)	.364 (2.94)	-.064 (.51)	-.056 (.46)	.121 (1.03)		.500	2.53 (5,15)	.46	.28	4.08	.80 (4,7)
Ecuador (1964–83)	.071 (.39)	.151 (.80)	-.023 (.13)	.350 (1.93)	.176 (.95)	-.003 (1.73)	.725	1.16 (6,13)	.35	.05	7.74	.96 (4,5)
Egypt (1962–83)	.319 (1.78)	.109 (.62)	.141 (.79)	.336 (1.89)	.078 (.41)		.983	1.95 (5,16)	.38	.18	10.61	1.97 (4,8)

114

Table 2—Continued

Country	B0	B1	B2	B3	B4	λ	X1	F	R^2	$\bar{R}^2$	Q-test	F-test
El Salvador (1963-83)	-.018 (.24)	.138 (1.63)	.281 (3.07)	.219 (2.54)	.052 (.60)	-.006 (5.97)	.672	8.71 (6,12)	.81	.72	3.43	3.06 (4,4)
Finland (1964-83)	.050 (.54)	.098 (1.10)	-.056 (.65)	-.158 (1.75)	-.058 (.59)		.148	1.02 (5,14)	.27	.005	10.5	.68 (4,6)
France (1964-83)	-.144 (1.30)	-.052 (.46)	-.039 (.37)	-.245 (2.00)	-.118 (1.01)	-.003 (5.13)	-.144	5.22 (6,13)	.71	.57	7.20	.84 (4,5)
Germany (1960-83)	-.03 (.23)	.360 (2.78)	.126 (.99)	-.154 (1.11)	-.234 (1.63)	-.002 (3.30)	.456	4.88 (6,17)	.63	.50	6.29	.81 (4,9)
Ghana (1965-83)	.023 (.19)	.057 (.52)	-.024 (.22)	-.158 (1.40)	-.065 (.57)		.080	.56 (5,13)	.18	-.14	4.02	.28 (4,5)
Greece (1962-83)	.074 (.42)	-.357 (1.93)	.059 (.32)	-.286 (1.58)	.096 (.56)	-.003 (3.15)	.074	2.71 (6,15)	.52	.33	2.05	.22 (4,7)
Guatemala (1964-82)	.218 (1.72)	.001 (.01)	.088 (.74)	-.076 (.61)	.179 (1.46)	-.003 (2.45)	.410	1.51 (6,12)	.43	.15	3.41	.09 (4,4)
Haiti (1963-83)	.069 (1.24)	.104 (1.87)	.061 (1.06)	.090 (1.58)	.108 (1.74)		.432	2.15 (5,15)	.42	.22	4.15	.50 (4,7)
Honduras (1963-83)	.334 (2.29)	.476 (2.90)	.236 (1.43)	.387 (2.43)	.195 (1.42)	-.002 (1.66)	1.598	2.63 (6,14)	.53	.33	11.14	1.09 (4,6)
Iceland (1964-83)	.218 (2.98)	.216 (2.76)	.067 (.81)	-.087 (1.09)	-.160 (1.96)	-.005 (3.79)	.501	6.24 (6,13)	.74	.62	4.76	.38 (10,5)
India (1964-82)	.065 (.13)	.095 (.23)	-.187 (.41)	-.145 (.36)	.017 (.04)		.160	.07 (5,13)	.02	-.35	4.23	.47 (4,5)
Ireland (1963-82)	.083 (1.29)	.132 (2.02)	.110 (1.53)	-.198 (2.76)	-.330 (4.60)		.325	7.38 (5,14)	.72	.63	12.39	.75 (4,6)

115

Table 2—Continued

Country	B0	B1	B2	B3	B4	λ	X1	F	R^2	$\bar{R}^2$	Q-test	F-test
Israel (1964–83)	.087 (.77)	.251 (2.13)	.140 (1.21)	-.063 (.54)	-.020 (.13)	-.003 (2.42)	.478	2.62 (6,13)	.55	.34	8.03	1.63 (4,5)
Italy (1962–82)	.040 (.29)	.200 (1.45)	-.108 (.78)	.153 (1.06)	-.011 (.07)	.003 (2.73)	.285	2.21 (6,15)	.47	.26	7.61	.32 (4,7)
Jamaica (1963–83)	.468 (2.19)	-.022 (.11)	-.236 (1.32)	.015 (.08)	-.313 (1.57)	-.004 (1.56)	.468	2.29 (6,14)	.50	.28	13.09	1.14 (4,6)
Japan (1962–83)	-.034 (.28)	-.030 (.23)	-.127 (1.04)	-.204 (1.58)	-.071 (.48)	-.004 (4.37)	-.034	3.91 (6,15)	.61	.45	7.96	.88 (4,7)
Korea (1964–83)	.077 (.73)	.312 (2.91)	.034 (.31)	-.042 (.41)	.171 (1.53)		.552	2.72 (5,14)	.49	.31	5.60	3.36* (4,6)
Malaysia (1961–83)	.427 (2.69)	.151 (.91)	-.167 (1.05)	.151 (.93)	.117 (.71)	.002 (1.12)	.679	2.69 (6,16)	.50	.32	5.92	1.37 (4,8)
Mexico (1964–83)	-.111 (.68)	-.304 (1.85)	-.025 (.10)	-.083 (.33)	.008 (.03)	-.003 (2.05)	-.111	1.59 (6,13)	.42	.16	7.96	3.97* (4,5)
Netherlands (1964–83)	.012 (.12)	.145 (1.35)	.208 (1.92)	-.072 (.59)	-.227 (1.91)	-.003 (3.67)	.365	4.99 (6,13)	.70	.56	6.60	1.75 (4,5)
Nigeria (1963–83)	.448 (4.26)	.134 (1.06)	-.045 (.37)	-.163 (1.21)	-.212 (1.89)		.582	4.98 (5,13)	.66	.52	6.38	.72 (4,5)
New Zealand (1961–82)	.090 (1.28)	.133 (2.11)	-.044 (.73)	.008 (.13)	-.100 (1.40)	-.002 (2.49)	.223	2.95 (6,15)	.54	.36	16.2*	.96 (4,7)
Norway (1964–83)	-.191 (1.49)	.069 (.55)	.158 (1.24)	.074 (.56)	.206 (1.33)	-.001 (1.57)	.316	1.51 (6,13)	.41	.14	3.74	1.01 (4,5)

116

Table 2—Continued

Country	B0	B1	B2	B3	B4	λ	X1	F	R^2	$\bar{R}^2$	Q-test	F-test
Panama (1963–83)	.043 (.49)	.013 (.15)	-.063 (.76)	-.083 (.99)	-.134 (1.60)		.056	.90 (5,15)	.23	-.03	16.79*	2.95 (4,7)
Paraguay (1960–83)	.152 (3.70)	.204 (5.11)	.067 (1.60)	-.005 (.12)	-.025 (.58)		.423	9.56 (5,18)	.73	.65	6.37	.65 (4,10)
Peru (1964–83)	.528 (1.59)	-.252 (.76)	-.208 (.65)	.055 (.17)	-.353 (1.13)	-.006 (2.05)	.528	1.66 (6,13)	.43	.17	8.78	1.26 (4,5)
Philippines (1960–83)	.065 (1.76)	.142 (3.52)	.105 (2.33)	-.021 (.42)	.037 (.75)		.328	4.27 (5,18)	.54	.42	5.87	.89 (4,10)
Portugal (1964–82)	-.026 (.17)	.039 (.26)	-.320 (2.16)	-.101 (.70)	.232 (1.61)	-.002 (1.81)	.013	2.40 (6,12)	.55	.32	9.15	.34 (4,4)
South Africa (1961–83)	-.003 (.04)	.100 (1.41)	.072 (1.09)	.073 (1.06)	-.196 (2.36)	-.003 (4.53)	.097	6.11 (6,16)	.70	.58	5.91	2.42 (4,8)
Spain (1962–83)	.112 (1.28)	.124 (1.35)	.013 (.15)	-.162 (1.98)	-.165 (1.99)	-.003 (4.62)	.249	12.63 (6,15)	.83	.77	6.57	.67 (4,7)
Sri Lanka (1963–83)	-.020 (.21)	-.081 (.84)	.017 (.18)	.034 (.35)	-.157 (1.60)		-.020	.71 (5,15)	.19	-.08	5.92	.35 (4,7)
Sweden (1961–83)	.053 (.76)	-.072 (.96)	-.076 (1.16)	.029 (.45)	-.009 (.12)	-.002 (6.14)	.053	8.85 (6,14)	.79	.70	5.00	.15 (4,6)
Switzerland (1964–83)	.043 (.23)	.145 (.83)	.320 (1.76)	.050 (.30)	-.313 (1.92)	-.002 (1.50)	.558	2.38 (6,13)	.52	.30	16.9*	1.15 (4,5)
Thailand (1962–83)	.070 (1.04)	.108 (1.47)	.097 (1.32)	.008 (.10)	-.045 (.58)	-.001 (2.25)	.283	1.68 (6,15)	.40	.16	8.39	.23 (4,7)
Trinidad & Tobago (1963–83)	.277 (1.31)	.236 (1.07)	.451 (2.16)	.325 (1.54)	-.254 (1.34)		1.289	6.75 (5,12)	.74	.63	4.35	3.24 (4,4)

Table 2—Continued

Country	B0	B1	B2	B3	B4	λ	X1	F	R^2	$\bar{R}^2$	Q-test	F-test
Turkey (1964–83)	-.195 (1.18)	-.357 (2.16)	.057 (.36)	-.176 (.98)	.012 (.07)	-.002 (1.51)	-.195	1.81 (6,13)	.45	.20	6.71	.65 (4,5)
United Kingdom (1964–83)	-.003 (.01)	.168 (.89)	-.047 (.30)	-.112 (.72)	-.097 (.63)		.165	.43 (5,14)	.13	-.18	6.62	.75 (4,6)
United States (1964–83)	.311 (.74)	.486 (1.15)	-.330 (.77)	-.877 (2.06)	-.023 (.05)	-.001 (1.17)	.797	1.95 (6,13)	.47	.23	14.7	4.59* (4,5)
Venezuela (1964–83)	.037 (.55)	.155 (2.36)	.256 (3.92)	.134 (1.97)	.014 (.22)	-.004 (4.89)	.596	8.12 (6,13)	.79	.69	6.88	1.07 (4,5)

Source: George Macesich and Munir A. S. Choudhary, "Cross-Country Tests of the Macro-Rational Expectations Hypothesis," unpublished manuscript.

Notes: RM is residuals from money supply equations given in Table 1. T is time trend variable. $X1 = MAX \sum_{i=0}^{4} Bi$. F is F-statistics to test whether all the variables in the equation are jointly insignificant. R^2 is R^2 adjusted for degree of freedom. Q-test is Box-Pierce statistics over ten residuals from output equation. F-test is Durbin-F statistics with degree of freedom in parentheses. t-statistics are given in parentheses under the estimated coefficients. Estimates reported for El Salvador, Nigeria, Sweden, Trinidad and Tobago are after the second-order autocorrelation in residuals was corrected using the Cochrane-Orcutt technique.

   *Specification rejected at 10 percent level.

  **Specification rejected at 5 percent level.

Table 3
Real Output Equation (Restricted OLS):

$$Y = CO + \sum_{i=0}^{4} BiRMt - i + \lambda T + Ut$$

Country	B0	B1	B2	B3	B4	λ	X2	F1
Australia (1964–83)	.009 (.13)	.089 (1.26)	-.147 (2.01)	.044 (.59)	.005 (.06)	-.216 (3.38)	.089	.47 (1,13)
Austria (1964–83)	-.008 (.11)	.147 (1.80)	-.044 (.55)	-.148 (1.78)	.053 (.65)	-.002 (3.00)	.139	1.15 (1,13)
Belgium (1961–83)	.017 (.13)	.182 (1.43)	.069 (.53)	-.212 (1.67)	-.056 (.41)	-.001 (1.64)	.268	.98 (1,16)
Bolivia (1963–83)	-.115 (2.47)	-.034 (.72)	.038 (.65)	.061 (.72)	.050 (.67)	-.005 (4.06)	-.111	3.31 (1,14)
Burma (1964–83)	.103 (.92)	-.288 (2.56)	.333 (2.92)	-.054 (.46)	-.094 (.91)	.003 (2.40)	.148	1.01 (1,13)
Canada (1962–83)	-.046 (1.04)	.059 (1.49)	-.018 (.44)	-.047 (1.18)	.052 (1.19)	-.003 (3.67)	.013	1.41 (1,15)
Colombia (1964–83)	.270 (2.00)	.131 (.91)	-.004 (.03)	-.018 (.12)	-.397 (2.78)	-.002 (2.47)	.401	.01 (1,13)
Denmark (1964–83)	.094 (.69)	.164 (.95)	-.389 (2.43)	.053 (.32)	.079 (.52)	-.002 (2.93)	.258	1.92 (1,13)

Table 3—Continued

Country	B0	B1	B2	B3	B4	λ	X2	F1
Dominican Republic (1962–82)	.035 (.32)	.265 (2.41)	-.168 (1.54)	-.160 (1.55)	.028 (.27)		.300	2.05 (1,15)
Ecuador (1964–83)	-.080 (.46)	-.002 (.01)	-.142 (.78)	.208 (1.18)	.016 (.09)	-.003 (1.30)	-.080	2.75 (1,13)
Egypt (1962–83)	.087 (.44)	-.091 (.46)	.019 (.09)	.164 (.81)	-.179 (.89)		.087	7.89 (1,16)
El Salvador (1963–83)	-.112 (1.02)	-.027 (.23)	.155 (1.16)	.064 (.54)	-.080 (.64)	-.005 (3.55)	.016	16.80 (1,12)
Finland (1964–83)	.065 (.73)	.123 (1.52)	-.030 (.39)	-.129 (1.64)	-.028 (.32)		.188	.39 (1,14)
France (1964–83)	-.040 (.39)	.079 (.83)	.064 (.64)	-.097 (.99)	-.005 (.05)	-.003 (4.34)	.103	3.06 (1,13)
Germany (1960–83)	-.042 (.36)	.350 (2.93)	.110 (1.12)	-.168 (1.37)	-.249 (2.03)	-.002 (3.29)	.418	.04 (1,17)
Ghana (1963–83)	.062 (.58)	.087 (.86)	.009 (.09)	-.126 (1.23)	-.031 (.30)		.158	.39 (1,13)
Greece (1962–83)	.174 (1.10)	-.287 (1.60)	.141 (.80)	-.222 (1.26)	.194 (1.31)	-.003 (3.19)	.174	1.11 (1,15)

Table 3—Continued

Country	B0	B1	B2	B3	B4	λ	X2	F1
Guatemala (1964–82)	.132 (1.10)	-.082 (.74)	.002 (.02)	-.148 (1.21)	.096 (.82)	-.002 (1.93)	.132	2.03 (1,12)
Haiti (1963–83)	.004 (.05)	.024 (.38)	-.040 (.65)	.005 (.08)	.007 (.10)		.028	9.95 (1,15)
Honduras (1963–83)	.072 (.49)	.084 (.70)	-.170 (1.50)	.016 (.13)	-.001 (.01)	-.002 (1.25)	.156	8.59 (1,14)
Iceland (1964–83)	.165 (2.42)	.151 (2.19)	.034 (.40)	-.131 (1.65)	-.219 (2.89)	-.004 (3.4)	.350	2.07 (1,13)
India (1964–83)	.107 (.25)	.128 (.34)	-.171 (.38)	-.115 (.31)	.052 (.14)		.235	.03 (1,13)
Ireland (1963–82)	.119 (2.05)	.169 (2.88)	.156 (2.58)	-.155 (2.48)	-.289 (4.56)		.444	1.19 (1,14)
Israel (1964–83)	.020 (.18)	.167 (1.58)	.071 (.64)	-.115 (.99)	-.143 (1.06)	-.004 (2.67)	.258	1.74 (1,13)
Italy (1962–83)	-.010 (.08)	.157 (1.23)	-.159 (1.31)	.099 (.78)	-.087 (.69)	-.002 (2.63)	.147	.55 (1,15)
Jamaica (1963–83)	.484 (2.44)	-.006 (.03)	-.220 (1.36)	.035 (.21)	-.293 (1.68)	-.004 (1.59)	.484	.04 (1,14)

Table 3—Continued

Country	B0	B1	B2	B3	B4	λ	X2	F1
Japan (1962–83)	.053 (.50)	.077 (.71)	-.054 (.48)	-.118 (1.02)	.043 (.35)	-.004 (4.26)	.130	1.59 (1,15)
Korea (1964–83)	-.031 (.25)	.198 (1.58)	.003 (.02)	-.172 (1.50)	.002 (.02)		.170	8.11 (1,14)
Malaysia (1961–83)	.346 (2.12)	.008 (.05)	-.331 (2.46)	-.003 (.02)	-.20 (.13)	.003 (1.43)	.354	2.75 (1,16)
Mexico (1964–83)	-.025 (.18)	-.219 (1.50)	.085 (.38)	.015 (.06)	.144 (.72)	-.002 (1.75)	-.025	.99 (1,13)
Netherlands (1964–83)	-.000 (.00)	.134 (1.38)	.193 (2.13)	-.086 (.79)	-.242 (2.36)	-.003 (3.82)	.327	.06 (1,13)
Nigeria (1963–83)	.432 (4.23)	.097 (.91)	-.090 (1.11)	-.206 (1.93)	-.234 (2.23)		.529	.27 (1,13)
New Zealand (1961–82)	.065 (1.11)	.122 (1.99)	-.060 (1.08)	-.000 (.00)	-.127 (2.18)	-.002 (2.39)	.187	.40 (1,15)
Norway (1964–83)	-.253 (2.19)	.010 (.09)	.086 (.80)	.017 (.14)	.139 (.97)	-.001 (1.75)	-.157	.97 (1,13)
Panama (1963–83)	.094 (1.15)	.066 (.81)	-.020 (.26)	-.045 (.55)	-.095 (1.16)		.160	1.53 (1,15)

Table 3—Continued

Country	B0	B1	B2	B3	B4	λ	X2	F1
Paraguay (1960–83)	.066 (1.16)	.146 (2.51)	-.005 (.08)	-.086 (1.42)	-.121 (2.07)		.212	23.89 (1,18)
Peru (1964–83)	.575 (2.10)	-.202 (.76)	-.162 (.62)	.098 (.37)	-.310 (1.19)	-.006 (2.05)	.575	.06 (1,13)
Philippines (1960–83)	.012 (.28)	.100 (2.06)	.036 (.71)	-.103 (1.92)	-.044 (.81)		.148	10.65 (1,13)
Portugal (1964–82)	.009 (.07)	.076 (.63)	-.283 (2.37)	-.066 (.56)	.264 (2.17)	-.002 (1.77)	.085	.18 (1,12)
South Africa (1961–83)	.052 (.92)	.150 (2.40)	-.048 (.73)	-.032 (.51)	-.121 (2.00)	-.002 (4.15)	.202	1.58 (1,16)
Spain (1962–83)	.123 (1.56)	.145 (2.21)	.031 (.47)	-.146 (2.29)	-.154 (2.04)	-.003 (6.11)	.299	.10 (1,15)
Sri Lanka (1963–83)	.020 (.22)	-.041 (.45)	.058 (.66)	.077 (.86)	-.114 (1.27)		.037	.91 (1,15)
Sweden (1961–83)	.068 (1.22)	-.056 (.88)	-.062 (1.12)	.043 (.81)	.007 (.11)	-.002 (6.56)	.068	.15 (1,14)
Switzerland (1964–83)	-.008 (.06)	.096 (.70)	.262 (2.02)	.001 (.01)	-.351 (2.50)	-.002 (1.62)	.350	.20 (1,13)

Table 3—Continued

Country	B0	B1	B2	B3	B4	λ	X2	F1
Thailand (1962–83)	.032 (.53)	.062 (.96)	.048 (.76)	-.042 (.64)	-.101 (1.60)	-.001 (1.84)	.142	1.38 (1,15)
Trinidad & Tobago (1963–82)	-.092 (3.0)	.109 (.31)	.500 (1.50)	.064 (.20)	-.582 (2.08)		.517	18.8 (1,12)
Turkey (1964–83)	-.076 (.50)	-.220 (1.54)	.174 (1.17)	-.022 (.14)	.144 (.86)	-.002 (1.71)	-.076	1.99 (1,13)
United Kingdom (1964–83)	.021 (.12)	.183 (1.01)	-.030 (.20)	-.098 (.66)	-.077 (.55)		.204	.41 (5,14)
United States (1964–83)	.392 (1.11)	.572 (1.64)	-.239 (.70)	-.789 (2.28)	.065 (.18)	-.001 (1.24)	.964	.12 (1,13)
Venezuela (1964–83)	-.076 (.84)	.078 (.83)	.123 (1.46)	-.001 (.01)	-.123 (1.44)	-.004 (3.00)	.125	16.19 (1,13)

Source: George Macesich and Munir A. S. Choudhary, "Cross-Country Tests of the Macro-Rational Expectations Hypothesis," unpublished manuscript.
Notes: RM is residuals from money supply equations given in Table 1. T is time trend variable, t-statistics are given in parentheses under the estimated coefficients. $X2 = \underset{i=0}{\text{Max}}^{2} \, Bi$. F1 is F-statistics to test whether the long-run neutrality holds; that is, $\sum_{i=0}^{4} Bi = 0$.

Figure 1
Cross-Country Evidence with Restricted OLS.

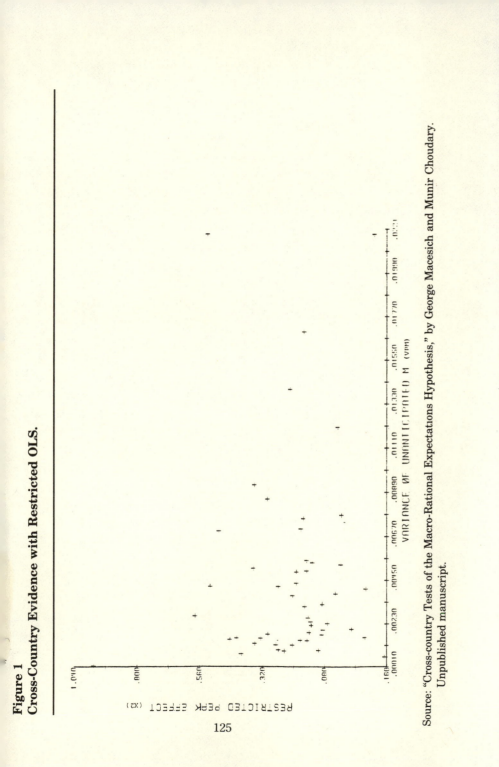

Source: "Cross-country Tests of the Macro-Rational Expectations Hypothesis," by George Macesich and Munir Choudary. Unpublished manuscript.

Figure 2
Cross-Country Evidence with Unrestricted OLS.

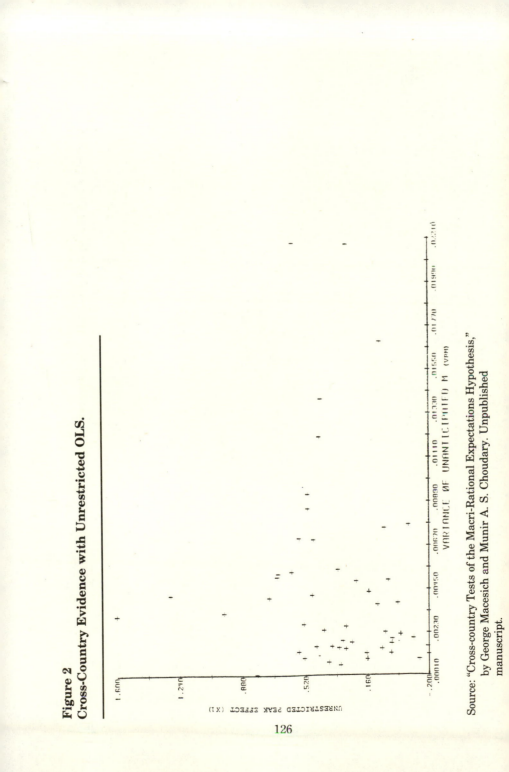

Source: "Cross-country Tests of the Macri-Rational Expectations Hypothesis,"
by George Macesich and Munir A. S. Choudary. Unpublished
manuscript.

126

CHAPTER 8

Prescription for Monetary Policy and Rational Expectations

THE PROBLEM

The problem confronted by policy makers is, whose advice do you rely upon in formulating and executing monetary policy? Shall they rely upon that of the now discredited Keynesians and their all but total disregard of expectations, rational or otherwise? Shall it be the advice of the main-line monetarists who have used rational expectations to undermine the one-time firm belief in the stability of the Keynesian Phillips-curve trade-off but find unacceptable the new classical view of rational expectations and its insistence that a fully anticipated money supply policy is ineffective? In short, shall it be the advice of the Keynesians that the cure for inflation and stability is not to be found in monetary policy only; shall it be the monetarist view of monetary policy of only a slow and gradual growth in the money supply within a rules-oriented policy system; or shall it be a quick and clean break to end inflationary monetary growth as the new classical school argues?

CRITICISM OF STANDARD MACRO MODEL EXPECTATIONS

The new classical macroeconomic models are not short on advice. Unfortunately, these models are not as simple and straightforward as the older macro models whereby a given change in some policy variable will produce an X percent rise in GNP with Y percent rise in prices. The new models say all of this too but add that it all depends upon the "state of expectations." But how is a policy maker to gauge the "state of expectations" and measure it quantitatively? Since such measures are notoriously unreliable, how does the policy maker select from alternative policies?

To be sure, most practitioners have attempted to deal with expectations, if not always successfully. Most are also aware that expectations affect all the parameters of the macroeconomic system. Many econometric model builders, for instance, consider themselves as working on the frontiers of new economic knowledge. Indeed, they insist that since the 1940s when the present generation of large econometric models (such as the Wharton Models) was being developed, expectations played a key role in the formulation of model structure.[1] Accordingly, the most important use of expectations occurs in model development through the use of sample survey information.

These model builders strongly deny that their forecasts and policy analyses have failed to keep pace with the role of expectations in economic theory. In their view when expected values are wanted in their econometric models they go to the source and measure these expectations by tabulating answers to questions posed to economic actors in sample surveys. Their models use indexes of consumer sentiment, expected purchases, expected income, and expected prices as measures of expectations by the public at large.

Detractors point out, however, that expectations have no known measurable weight or duration so that the whole concept and influence upon the course of the economy remains very subjective and vague. Even in sophisticated markets, so the argument goes, expectations shift constantly and analytical evaluations are sharply divergent. Even given government policy, it is difficult to judge and assign weight to foreign events, political upheavals, or natural disasters. There is no "one number" to summarize expectations or indeed their meaning. Moreover, there remains the suspicion that people answer questions about expectations very lightly indeed. In addition, answers themselves may well be sensitive to the wording of the question. These are among the more obvious questions raised about the validity of expectation surveys.

In the case of consumption in the United States, the findings from the Michigan Survey Research Center are used to approximate expectations about the future levels of household income. In the case of investment, stock market prices are used to gauge expectations about future business profitability. In both cases, the effort to incorporate expectations into the analysis explicitly led to little or no improvement in the ability to model the behavior of business firms and households. Despite questions raised about these expectation surveys, examination of the Michigan Survey Center studies shows them to be reasonable and useful. The Center is correct in promoting and studying the formation of expectations and improving the methodology of such surveys.

In addition to survey data, expectations can be measured in other ways. For instance, econometric equations that infer expectations from the behavior of measurable data such as interest rates or wage changes are used in some studies. In other studies broad historical analyses are used.

Perhaps most important in terms of their use are expectations formed from past experience. This is in the nature of the learning process itself, which may be slow thanks to the difficulties of extracting accurate information from limited and very brief data. This may also be an advantage since it allows experience to accumulate before any precipitous action is undertaken.

Other important sources of information on expectations are prices and quantities transacted in markets where actions reflect expectations. Thus the expectation of inflation must affect interest rates. Given a theory of how expectations affect interest rates, it is possible to estimate expectations from observed interest rates. Of course, there must always be a theory between the observed facts such as nominal interest rates and the implied expectations.

As useful as it is to have better and regularly conducted data surveys of the expectations of households and firms, such efforts will not likely resolve the existing controversies and uncertainties regarding the role of expectations as viewed by new classical economists.[2] It is not the answers given by households and firms to questions asked in surveys that are relevant for economics, but the way in which views of the future affect supply and demand decisions of households and firms. Private agents take account of expected future developments but do not necessarily take into explicit account magnitudes of variables to prevail in the future when they make their supply and demand decisions. Consequently, there are really no records as such to which one can turn for answers to questions asked in surveys, and, of course, nothing to induce conformance between actual and reported expectations, and it is doubtful that additional data, however carefully gathered, will do much to resolve the issue of expectations.

The point is that expectational theories suggest that agents act *as if* they formed explicit expectations according to some criterion as rationality. These theories, however, do not imply that such agents are explicitly aware of their expectational magnitudes any more than traditional economic theory implies that firms are explicitly aware of their marginal revenue and marginal cost functions at any given moment of time. There is thus nothing inconsistent about the argument that assigns expectations a primary role and yet argues that agents are not necessarily able to provide accurate answers to questions regarding their expectations. This is also correct even if the argument asserts that expectations are formed rationally and thus without systematic errors.

A useful illustration of why expectations about the future affect decisions made today is provided by Milton Friedman's analysis of the determinants of how much of a household's current income it wishes to save for the future. Thus, the more a household earns the more it will it tend to spend. Friedman's point, however, is that current expenditures for the household depend not only on current income but also on expected future income. If a household expects to earn more in the future it will also tend to spend more today. Life expectancy, anticipated future earnings, and indeed expected future tax payments will tend to influence a household's decisions about how much to spend now and how much to save. This also holds true for a firm when it considers and makes its investment decisions. For instance, a firm will weigh the present cost of a piece of machinery against the additional profits it expects such equipment to generate over its productive lifetime. As a result, forecasts about the future demand for the firm's product and the price at which the product will sell are an essential element in a rational investment decision. As with the household, the firm will have expectations about the future that will influence its investment decision. Such factors as future tax policy, government regulation, and a host of other assorted factors will influence its expectation regarding the future.

STATUS OF STANDARD MODELS

What then is the status of the current standard macroeconomic and macroeconometric models? Can they be renovated to take into account the new developments in expectations? The answer, according to the new classical views, is no. The deficiencies in the standard models cannot be remedied simply by adding a few extra equations or a few variables as their sponsors argue. They are basically flawed because of the manner in which the expectations foundations are constructed in these models.

This is certainly at odds with the views held and advanced by the proponents of standard large-scale econometric models as noted above—Wharton model, Klein-Goldberger model including FMP, Brookings, DRI, Chase, and UCLA models of the American economy. Their critics brush aside such remonstrations. They insist that these models simply do not accurately depict the way in which agents form expectations or the way in which their supplies and demands will respond to various policy measures. As a result they are not very useful for conditional forecasting, that is, forecasting conditional upon various assumptions regarding governmental policy. Any important change in policy will lead to changes in agents' supply-demand behavior that will not be taken into account by the equations of the model. Consequently, information about the effects of policy changes derived from large-scale econometric models will be inaccurate. These prediction errors, moreover, will not be random. Indeed, the models' forecasts will be systematically incorrect.

If these large models are used for prediction, it is assumed that the policy to be followed is not significantly different from the one in force when the model was designed and estimated. If significant changes in the direction and emphasis of, say, monetary and fiscal policy do occur, the foregoing justification is inapplicable. It is after all nonsense to argue that we can accurately predict the effects of major policy changes with a tool that assumes no important change has taken place.[3]

In sum, the existing large-scale econometric models, which are in turn based on standard macroeconomic models, cannot accurately predict the effects of major policy changes. According to the critics, replacement models must take into explicit account expectations and should incorporate the hypothesis that expectations of private agents are rational. Expectations cannot be manipulated independent of reality. Statements about what people reply to in survey studies or about what policy makers hope will happen, dressed up in the form of predictions, are unlikely to have a serious effect on expectations, particularly if other information is available to agents acting in their own self-interest.

EXPECTATIONS: ADAPTIVE OR RATIONAL?

It is useful to consider briefly how expectations are formed. This appears to be the key issue in the role of expectations in economics. The traditional and standard macroeconomic model proceeds on the assumption that agents form expectations of future events according to a given simple rule. Thus the value of a variable, say X, that agents expect to observe in the coming period is simply a weighted average of the values of X that have been observed during the previous periods. Both the values of the (a_i) and the order of the weighted sum (n) are either based on statistical procedures or arbitrarily selected by the model's constructors. The general class of these expectation models is called "autoregressive" (AR) since the expected future values of X are based simply on the past values of X.

To be sure, AR models are an improvement over static models. As a class of expectations models, however, they are generally too restrictive. These models assume that whatever information an agent may have about future values of X it is restricted to its past values. Moreover, AR models may at times not make full use of available information. For instance, an agent may have information about the future course of other variables that are known to be systematically related to X. In such cases AR models can be interpreted as assuming that agents do not make full use of potentially valuable information.

AR models of expectation formulation are widely used in economic analyses and policy. Their attractiveness to economists and others is their obvious mathematical simplicity and their aggreable assumption, to many economists at least, that agents form their expectations from relatively simple and stable forecasting schemes. Future rates of inflation, for instance, are supposed to be forecast by simple extrapolations of the behavior of inflation in the recent past. That is, agents form their expectations in an "adaptive" manner.

Unfortunately, "adaptive expectations" schemes are plagued by a number of shortcomings. Agents, for one, are not as naive about how inflation, unemployment, and output are determined. They do not ignore the interactions of a modern economy in such issues as the money supply, inflation, employment, and output. As a result "adaptive expectations" schemes typically produce economic forecasts that are persistently erroneous.

Moreover, agents who act in their own best interests would simply not form expectations adaptively. Such agents would use all the information they have available in the most efficient manner. Indeed this observation led John Muth as early as 1961 to propose the alternative hypothesis of "rational expectations."

In essence, the "rational expectations" hypothesis as formulated by Muth argues that agents do indeed use all the information they have available in the most efficient manner. Such information would include not only past behavior of the economic variable being forecast but also the past behavior of other economic variables that interact with that variable as well as any other information agents have about what they think might happen in the future.

This does not mean, of course, that rational expectations are never wrong or that forecasting errors can be avoided. The uncertain nature of the real world would quickly repudiate any such claims. It does mean that systematic mistakes can be avoided. For this reason they are superior to adaptive expectations that do lead to systematic errors because not all available information is used.

Thus it is that in coming to grips with inflation in the 1970s, the late-1960s versions of the large traditional econometric models based largely on adaptive expectations grossly underestimated what actually happened to rates of inflation, unemployment, and output. For instance, these models predicted that a sustained rate of unemployment of 4 percent would be consistent with an annual rate of inflation of 4 percent. The evidence, however, indicates that in each of the years from 1970 to 1973 and before the OPEC crisis both unemployment and inflation were significantly higher than the amounts suggested by the traditional large macroeconometric models.

Nor indeed were these models stable. Thus addition of new data in the 1970s did nothing to maintain user confidence in these models. In fact the estimates produced were significantly different from actual values. This suggested that the structure of the economy had changed so that the initial specifications of the models were no longer appropriate. Nor indeed were such complicated ad hoc "add factors" much help in improving the performance of the models.

These models, unfortunately, had serious consequences for public policy. They had the effect of creating an illusion that inflation was somehow an integral part of the economic structure. In these adaptive expectations models, inflation projections are little more than extrapolations of previous inflation trends with allowance for the effects of changes in unemployment rates, capacity utilization, and other short-term market conditions. In effect, if monetary policy and fiscal policy were to have any effect on inflation they would be required to be restrictive for a very long time, since the lower inflation rates would need to pass through the parameters of the adaptive expectations process and so to alter significantly the momentum in the inflation process.

Policy makers were erroneously advised by the users of such models that halting inflation would place unbearable costs on society in terms of unemployment and output losses. As a result monetary and fiscal policies in most industrialized countries had an inflationary bias. They were, moreover, misguided into believing that "income policies," including wage and price controls, could be used to bring down inflation rates by breaking the psychology of inflation. Such "stop and go" policies simply have not worked as a means for controlling inflation.

The rational expectations hypothesis, however, is not just another way of modeling how agents forecast the future. Indeed if this were the case the hypothesis could be added to the existing macro models in place of the adaptive expectations hypothesis. According to Robert Lucas in his now well-known criticism of standard macroeconomics, rational expectations is a far more serious challenge. Economists must simply, according to Lucas, reconsider the entire way in which economic models are formulated. His discussion focuses on agents' decision rules that express their economic behavior in terms of those factors on which their behavior depends. Lucas's analysis attempts to show that changes in the general economic environment within which agents carry out their ongoing affairs, say in changes in the money supply, would result in changes in the entire form of these decision rules. In essence, changes in the "rules of the game" in which agents participate will impact upon the economic behavior of agents. Since behavior does depend upon the "rules of the game," economists must significantly change the way economic models are formulated and used to assess the effects of alternative government policies when these rules change.

In effect, Lucas's contribution may be summed up by the observation that if expectations are rational, then the parameters of standard macroeconomic models will not be invariant to policy change. Thus even though standard models might serve as a useful summary of the way things have been in the past, and may provide useful projections about the path the economy would take if policy maintained its historical course, they are of little use in assessing the likely course of the economy if policy were changed. Choosing economic policies based on comparisons of simulations from standard models is in effect a misleading venture. Thomas Sargent, Neil Wallace, Robert Barro, and others have joined in raising doubts about the usefulness of standard macroeconomic models.

Moreover, the rational expectations hypothesis does not assume that agents are possessed of perfect foresight, as some critics argue. It simply states that there is no sound theoretical reason for restricting an agent's information sets to historical values of the "own" series as in the adaptive expectations hypothesis. The rational expectations hypothesis leaves the choice of agent's information sets to the modeler subject to the condition that *ex ante* agents possess the same information about the structure of the model as does the modeler. The net effect is to constrain severely the options open to the modeler.

Such constraints do not allow the modeler free rein to assume any level of detail about the structure of the overall model without violating the assumed expectations process. For instance, a modeler cannot assume circumstances, conditions, and information not available to the economic agent. An example will illustrate the issue. A modeler cannot construct a model for a market for commodity X, which depends not only on the price for X but also on consumer incomes and prices for complementary goods, while requiring that agents in the model (producers of X) forecast future prices by extrapolating only the recent price of X. In short, the modeler makes only one choice for the structure of the model that is chosen by the modeler and also represents the information set available to agents with the model.

The issue may be illustrated with yet another example. Patterns of human behavior depend very much on the rules of the game. Change in the rules of the game would also change the pattern of human behavior as a result. If the entire tax system were to change, for example, the rational expectations hypothesis implies that the very way people plan their spending and saving would change. Current spending can still depend upon current income. Its precise relationship, however, would in general be quite different after the change in tax rates. Past behavior of agents will not be a reliable guide to future behavior because the rules of the game have now changed. In a changing economic environment wherein the rules of the game are also changing, historically based patterns of behavior may indeed be a poor guide for the construction of stable macroeconomic models. Unlike actions taken against inanimate subjects, human subjects do react to actions taken by policy makers.

The fact that agents do look forward in making their decisions has important implications for the way policy makers think of and attempt to design suitable macroeconomic policy. If expectation decisions are taken seriously, it becomes necessary for government policy to be accurately and easily predictable. The best way to achieve this is for the government to follow well-understood policy rules. Thanks to its large size relative to individual agents, government does have a special responsibility to act clearly, predictably, and consistently. It is absolutely essential for private decision making that the government follow a widely understood and predictable rule.

The primary objective of good economic policy may well be predictability, since agents do make decisions that are forward-looking. The rational expectations hypothesis suggests that predictability in government policy is essential because it facilitates the making of forecasts by private agents. Good private-agent forecasts are mutually advantageous for the effective and productive operation of the economy.

The implications for the conduct of monetary policy are straightforward. Given that monetary aggregates are viewed by agents as important sources of swings in aggregate demand, monetary policy is an important factor influencing expectations. For this reason monetary policy should be based on policy rules that are publicly announced and adhered to. Such an arrangement will assure that monetary authorities act in a clear, predictable, and consistent manner. On this fundamental and important issue of rules versus discretionary authority the new classical school and the rational expectations hypothesis are in agreement with the old-style monetarists.[4]

NOTES

1. See, for instance, L. R. Klein, *Economic Fluctuations in the United States, 1921–1941* (New York: John Wiley, 1950).

2. See, for instance, the views on rational expectations expressed in Stanley Fischer, ed., *Rational Expectations and Economic Policy* (Chicago: University of Chicago Press, for NBER, 1980); and *Journal of Money, Credit and Banking*, November 1980. See also Robert E. Lucas, Jr. and Thomas J. Sargent, eds., *Rational Expectations and Econometric Practice* (Minneapolis: University of Minnesota Press, 1981).

3. For a useful discussion of these and related issues, see Bennett T. McCallum, "Topics Concerning the Formulation, Estimation, and Use of Macroeconomic Models with Rational Expectations," American Statistical Association, 1979 Proceedings of the Business and Economic Statistics Section, pp. 65–72.

4. George Macesich, *The Politics of Monetarism: Its Historical and Institutional Development* (Totawa, N.J.: Rowman and Allenheld, 1984).

Selected Bibliography

Alberro, J. 1981. "The Lucas Hypothesis on the Phillips Curve: Further International Evidence," *Journal of Monetary Economics* 7, (March): 239–50.

Attfield, C. and N. Duck. 1983. "The Influence of Unanticipated Money Growth on Real Output: Some Cross-Country Estimates." *Journal of Money, Credit and Banking* 15, (November): 442–54.

Azariadis, C. 1973. "Implicit Contracts and Underdevelopment Equilibria." *Journal of Political Economy* 83, (December): 1183, 1202.

Baily, M. N. 1974. "Wages and Employment Under Uncertain Demand." *Review of Economic Studies* 41, (January): 119–55.

———. 1983. "The Labour Market in the 1930's." In *Macro Economics, Prices and Quantities*, edited by J. Tobin. Washington, D. C.: The Brookings Institution.

Barro, R. J. 1976. "Rational Expectations and the Role of Monetary Policy." *Journal of Monetary Economics* 2, (January): 1095–1117.

———. 1977a. "Unanticipated Money Growth and Unemployment in the United States." *American Economic Review* 67, (March): 101–15.

———. 1977b. "Long-term Contracting Sticky Prices, and Monetary Policy." *Journal of Monetary Economics* 3, (July): 305–16.

———. 1978. "Unanticipated Money, Output, and Price Level in the United States." *Journal of Political Economy* 86, (August): 549–80.

———. 1979. "On the Determination of the Public Debt." *Journal of Political Economy* 87, (October): 940–71.

———. 1981. "Unanticipated Money Growth and Economic Activity in the United States." In *Money Expectations and Business Cycles*, edited by R. J. Barro. New York: Academic Press.

Barro, R. J. and M. Rush. 1980. "Unanticipated Money and Economic Activity." In *Rational Expectations and Economic Policy*, edited by S. Fischer. Chicago: University of Chicago Press.

Barro, R. J. and David Gordon. 1983a. "Rules, Discretion and Reputation in a Model of Monetary Policy." *Journal of Monetary Economics* 12, (July): 101–12.

———. 1983b. "A Positive Theory of Monetary Policy in a Natural-Rate Model." *Journal of Political Economy* 91, (August): 589–610.

Batten, R. J. and R. W. Hafer. 1983. "The Relative Impact of Monetary and Fiscal Actions on Economic Activity: A Cross-Country Comparison." *Federal Reserve Bank of St. Louis Review* 65, 5–12.

Boothe, P., K. Clinton, A. Coté, and D. Longworth. 1985 *International Asset Substitutability: Theory and Evidence for Canada*. Ottawa: Bank of Canada, February.

Claassen, Emil, and Charles Wyplosz. 1982. "Capital Controls: Some Principles and the French Experience." *Annales de l'INSEE* 47–48, (June–December 1982): 237–67.

Cornell, Bradford. 1983a. "Money Supply Announcements and Interest Rates: Another View." *Journal of Business* 56, (January): 1–24.

———. 1983b. "The Money Supply Announcement Puzzle: Review and Interpretations." *American Economic Review* 75, (June): 565–66.

Crockett, A. D. 1982. "Stabilization Policies in Developing Countries: Some Policy Considerations." *IMF Staff Papers* 29: 54–79.

Culbertson, John M. 1968. *Macroeconomic Theory and Stabilization Policy*. New York: McGraw-Hill: 545.

Cumby, R. 1984. "International Interest Rate and Price Level Linkages under Flexible Exchange Rates: A Review of Recent Evidence." In *Exchange Rate Theory and Practice*, edited by J. Bilson and R. Marston. Chicago: University of Chicago Press.

David, Paul, and John Scadding. 1974. "Private Savings: Ultrarationality, Aggregation and 'Denison's Law.' " *Journal of Political Economy* 82 (March-April): 225–49.

Dimitrijevic, Dimitrije, and George Macesich. 1984. *Money and Fi-*

nance in Yugoslavia: A Comparative Analysis New York: Praeger.

Dooley, Michael, and Peter Isard. 1980. "Capital Controls, Political Risk and Deviations from Interest-Rate Parity." *Journal of Political Economy* 88, (April): 360–84.

Dornbusch, Rudiger. 1983. "Exchange Rate Determination." In *The Internationalization of Financial Market and National Economic Policy*, edited by R. Hawkins, R. Levich, and C. Wihlborg. Greenwich, Conn.: JAI Press, 3–27.

Engel, Charles, and Jeffrey A. Frankel. 1984. "Why Money Supply Announcements Move Interest Rates: An Answer from the Foreign Exchange Market." *Journal of Monetary Economics* 13, (January): 31–40.

Erhard, Ludwig. 1963. *The Economics of Success*. Princeton, N.J.: Van Nostrand.

Fair, R. C. 1978, "A Criticism of One Class Macroeconomic Models with Rational Expectations." *Journal of Money, Credit and Banking* 10, (November): 411–17.

———. 1979. "An Analysis of the Accuracy of Four Macroeconomic Models." *Journal of Political Economy* 87, (August): 701–18.

Falk, Barry, and Peter F. Orazem. 1985. "The Money Supply Announcements Puzzle: Comment." *American Economic Review* 75, (June): 562–64.

Fase, M. M. G. 1976. "The Interdependence of Short-Term Interest Rates in the Major Financial Centers of the World: Some Evidence for 1961–1972." *Kyklos* 29, 63–96.

Feldstein, M. S. 1976. "Temporary Layoffs in the Theory of Unemployment." *Journal of Political Economy* 84, (October): 927–957.

Fischer, Stanley. 1977. "Long-term Contracts, Rational Expectations and the Optimal Money Supply Rules." *Journal of Political Economy* 85, (February): 191–205.

———. 1979. "Anticipations and the Non-neutrality of Money." *Journal of Political Economy* 87, (April): 225–52.

———. 1980. *Rational Expectations and Economic Policy*. University of Chicago Press for NBER.

Friedman, Milton. 1966. "What Price Guideposts?" In *Guidelines: Informal Controls and Market Places*, edited by F.P. Schultz and R. Z. Aliber. Chicago: University of Chicago Press. 17–39.

———. 1970. *The Counter-Revolution in Monetary Theory*. First Wincott Memorial Lecture. London: Institute of Economic Affairs.

————. 1972a. "Have Monetary Policies Failed?" *The American Economic Review* 62, (May): 11–18.

————. 1972b. "Comments on the Critics." *Journal of Political Economy* 80, (Sept.-Oct.): 906–50.

————. 1976. "Statement on the Conduct of Monetary Policy." In *Current Issues in Monetary Theory and Policy*, edited by T. M. Harilesky and J. T. Boorman. Arlington Heights, Ill: A.H.M. Publishing.

————. 1977. "Nobel Lecture: Inflation and Unemployment." *Journal of Political Economy* 85, (June): 451–72.

Friedman, Milton, and D. Meiselman. 1963. "The Relative Stability of Monetary Velocity and the Investment Multiplier in the United States." In *Commission on Money and Credit Stabilization Policies*. Englewood Cliffs, N.J.: Prentice-Hall.

Friedman, Milton, and A. Schwartz. 1963. *A Monetary History of the United States, 1867–1960*. Washington, D.C.: National Bureau of Economic Research.

————. 1982. *Money, Interest Rates and Prices in the United States and United Kingdom: 1867–1975*. Chicago: University of Chicago Press.

Galbraith, John. 1981. "Up from Monetarism and Other Wishful Thinking." *New York Review of Books* (August 13, 1982): 27–32.

Golden, David G., and James M. Poterba. 1980. "The Price of Popularity: The Political Business Cycles Reexamined." *American Journal of Political Science* 24, (November): 696–714.

Grossman, Jacob. 1981. "The Rationality of Money Supply Expectations and the Short-Run Response of Interest Rates to Monetary Surprises." *Journal of Money, Credit and Banking* 13, (November): 409–24.

Guisinger, S. E. 1981. "Stabilization Policies in Pakistan: The 1970–77 Experience." In *Economic Stabilization Policies in Developing Countries*, edited by W. R. Cline and S. Weintraub, Washington, D. C.: Brookings Institution.

Hall, R. 1975. "The Rigidity of Wages and the Persistence of Unemployment." *Brookings Papers on Economic Activity* vol 2, 301–35.

Hardouvelis, Gikas. 1984. "Market Perceptions of Monetary Policy and the Weekly Monetary Announcements." *Journal of Monetary Economics* 14, (September): 225–40.

Hartman, David. 1984. "The International Financial Market and U.S. Interest Rates." *Journal of International Money and Finance* 3, (April): 91–103.

Hayek, F. A. 1933. *Monetary Theory and the Trade Cycle*. New York: Harcourt, Brace and Company.

——. 1939. *Profits, Interest and Investment*. London: George Routledge and Sons.

——. 1979. *A Tiger by the Tail: The Keynesian Legacy of Inflation*. San Francisco: Cato Institute.

Hibbs, Douglass A., and Heino Fassbender, eds. 1981. *Contemporary Political Economy*, New York: North Holland.

Hoover, Kevin D. 1984. "Two Types of Monetarism." *Journal of Economic Literature*, 22, (March): 58–76.

Judd, John J. 1984. "Money Supply Announcements, Forward Interest Rates and Budget Deficits." *Federal Reserve Bank of San Francisco Economic Review* 4, (Fall): 36–46.

Keynes, J. M. 1943. "The Objective of International Monetary Stability." *The Economic Journal* (June–September): 185–87.

Kirchgassner, Gebhard. 1985. "Rationality, Casuality and the Relation between Economic Conditions and the Popularity of Parties: An Empirical Investigation for the Federal Republic of Germany, 1971–1982." *European Economic Review* 28, (June–July): 243–68.

Knight, Frank. 1937. *Risk Uncertainty and Profit*. London: London School of Economics.

Lerner, A. P. 1980. "A Non-Monetarist View of the Nature of Stagflation and a Plan for Mobilizing the Market Mechanism to Cure It." *Social Research* 47, (Summer): 339–51.

Loyes, Jan G. 1985. "Changing Interest Rate Responses to Money Supply Announcements: 1977–1983." *Journal of Monetary Economics* 15, (May): 323–32.

Lucas, Robert E. 1972. "Econometric Testing of the Natural Rate Hypothesis." In *The Economics of Price Determination Conference*. Washington, D.C.: Board of Governors, Federal Reserve System, pp. 50–59.

——. 1973. "Some International Evidence on Output-Inflation Trade-Offs." *American Economic Review* 63, (June): 326–34.

——. 1975. "An Equilibrium Model of the Business Cycle." *Journal of Political Economy* 83, (December): 1113–44.

——. 1977. "Understanding Business Cycles." In *Stabilization of the Domestic and International Economy*, edited by K. Brunner and Allan H. Meltzer. Carnegie-Rochester Conference Series, Vol. 5. Amsterdam: North Holland.

——. 1978. "Unemployment Policy." *American Economic Review* 68, (June): 353–57.

————. 1981. *Studies in Business Cycle Theory.* Oxford: Blacknell, M.I.T.

Lucas, R. E., Jr., and L. A. Rapping. 1970. "Real Wages, Employment and Inflation." In *Microeconomic Foundations of Employment, and Inflation Theory,* edited by E. S. Phelps. New York: W. W. Norton, 257–305.

Lucas, Robert E., Jr., and Thomas J. Sargent. eds. 1981. *Rational Expectations and Econometric Practice.* Minneapolis: University of Minnesota Press. 2 Vols.

Macesich, G. 1981. *The International Monetary Economy and the Third World.* New York: Praeger.

————. 1983. *Monetarism: Theory and Policy.* New York: Praeger.

————. 1984. *The Politics of Monetarism: Its Historical and Institutional Development.* Totowa, New Jersey: Roman and Allenheld.

Macesich, G. and H. L. Tsai. 1982. *Money in Economic Systems.* New York: Praeger.

Mankiw, N. Gregory, David E. Runkle, and Mathew D. Shapiro. 1984. "Are Preliminary Announcements of the Money Stock Rational Forecasts?" *Journal of Monetary Economics* 14, (July): 15–28.

Mayer, T. 1978. *The Structure of Monetarism.* New York: W.W. Norton.

McCallum, B. T. 1976. "Rational Expectations and the Natural Rate Hypothesis." *Econometrica* 44, (January): 43–52.

————. 1977. "Price Level Stickiness and the Feasibility of Monetary Stabilization with Rational Expectations." *Journal of Political Economy* 85, (June): 627–34.

————. 1979. "The Current State of the Policy-Ineffectiveness Debate." *American Economic Review* 69, (March): 240–45.

————. 1980. "Rational Expectations and Macroeconomic Stabilization Policy." *Journal of Money, Credit and Banking* 12, (November): 716–46.

————. 1982. "Macroeconomics After a Decade of Rational Expectations: Some Critical Issues." *Federal Reserve Bank of Richmond Economic Review* 68, (December): 3–12.

McCallum, B., and J. Whitaker. 1979. "The Effectiveness of Fiscal Feedback Rules and Automatic Stabilizers Under Rational Expectations." *Journal of Monetary Economics* 5, (April): 171–86.

Meltzer, A. 1982. "Is the Federal Reserve's Monetary Control Policy Misdirected?" *Journal of Money, Credit and Banking* (February): 146.

Mishkin, Frederick. 1984. "Are Real Interest Rates Equal Across Countries? An Empirical Investigation of International Parity Conditions." *Journal of Finance* 39, (December): 1345–58.

Modigliani, F. 1977. "The Monetarist Controversy or, Should We Forsake Stabilization Politics?" *American Economic Review* 67, (March): 1–19.

Modigliani, F., and A. Ando. 1980. "Impacts of Fiscal Actions on Aggregate Income and the Monetarist Controversy: Theory and Evidence." In *The Collected Papers of Franco Modigliani*, edited by A. Abel. 1, 142–67.

Muth, J. F. 1961. "Rational Expectations and the Theory of Price Movements." *Econometrica* 29, (June): 315–35.

Nordhaus, William D. 1975. "The Political Business Cycle." *Review of Economic Studies* 42, (April): 169–90.

Okun, A. M. 1981. *Prices and Quantities: A Macroeconomic Analysis.* Washington, D.C.: Brookings Institution.

Penati, Alessandro, and Michael Dooley. 1984. "Current Account Imbalances and Capital Formation in Industrial Countries, 1949–1981." *IMF Staff Papers* 31, (March): 1–24.

Reder, Melvin W. 1982. "Chicago Economics: Permanence and Change." *Journal of Economic Literature* 20, (March): 1–38.

Riley, John G. 1979. "Informational Equilibrium." *Econometrica* 47, (March): 331–59.

Roley, V. Vance. 1982. "Weekly Money Supply Announcements and the Volatility of Short-Term Interest Rates." *Federal Reserve Bank of Kansas City Economic Review* 67, (April): 3–15.

———. 1983. "The Response of Short-Term Interest-Rates to Weekly Money Announcements." *Journal of Money, Credit and Banking* 15, (August): 334-54.

Roley, V. Vance, and Rick Troll. 1983. "The Impact of New Economic Information on the Volatility of Short-Term Interest Rates." *Federal Reserve Bank of Kansas City Economic Review* 68, (February): 3–15.

Roley, V. Vance, and Carl E. Walsh. 1984. "Unanticipated Money and Interest Rates." *American Economic Review* (Papers and Proceedings) 74, (May): 49–54.

Sachs, J. 1981. "The Current Account and Macroeconomic Adjustment in the 1970's." *Brookings Papers on Economic Activity* 12, 201–68.

———. 1983. "Aspects of the Current Account Behavior of OECD Economies." In *Recent Issues in the Theory of Flexible Exchange Rates*, edited by E. Claassen and P. Salin. Amsterdam: North Holland.

Sargent, T. J. 1981. "Rational Expectations and the Dynamics of Hyperinflation." *International Economic Review* 14, (June): 328–50.

Sargent, T. J. and N. Wallace. 1973. "Rational Expectations and the Real Rate of Interest and the Natural Rate of Unemployment." In *Rational Expectations and Econometric Practice*, edited by Robert E. Lucas., Jr., and T. J. Sargent. Minneapolis: University of Minnesota Press, 158–98.

———. 1976. "Rational Expectations and the Theory of Economic Policy." *Journal of Monetary Economics* 12, (April): 169–83.

Schwartz, Anna J. 1969. "Short-Term Targets of Three Foreign Central Banks." In *Targets and Indicators of Monetary Policy*, edited by Karl Brunner, San Francisco: Chandler. 20–25.

Sheehey, E. J. 1984. "The Neutrality of Money in the Short-Run: Some Tests." *Journal of Money, Credit and Banking* 16, (May): 237–41.

Shiller, Robert J., John Y. Campbell, and Kermit Schoelholts. 1983. "Forward Rates and Future Policy: Interpreting the Term Structure of Interest Rates." *Brookings Paper on Economic Activity* 1, 173–217.

Small, D. H. 1979. "Unanticipated Money Growth and Unemployment in the United States: Comment." *American Economic Review* 69, (December):996–1003.

Smith, Adam. 1976. *An Inquiry into the Nature and Causes of the Wealth of Nations* Chicago, Ill: University of Chicago Press.

Tobin, J., and W. Buiter. 1982a. "Deficit Spending and Crowding Out in Shorter and Longer Runs." In *Essays in Economics*, edited by J. Tobin. 161–235. Cambridge, Mass.: M.I.T. Press.

———1982b. "Long-Run Effects of Fiscal Monetary Policy on Aggregate Demand." In *Essays in Economics*, edited by J. Tobin. 161–235. Cambridge, Mass.: M.I.T. Press.

Tobin, J. 1983. "Comments on Domestic Saving and International Capital Movements in the Long Run and the Short Run." *European Economic Review* 21, (March–April): 153–56.

Triffin, R. 1964. *The Evolution of the International Monetary System: Reappraisal of the International Monetary System: Reappraisal and Further Perspectives*. 12. Princeton, N.J.: Princeton Studies in International Finance.

Tufte, Edward R. 1978. *Political Control of the Economy*. Princeton, N.J.: Princeton University Press.

Turnovsky, S. J. 1972. "The Expectations Hypothesis and the Aggregate Wage Equation: Some Empirical Evidence for Canada." *Economica* 39, (February): 1–17.

————. 1980. "The Choice of Monetary Instruments under Alternative Forms of Price Expectations." *Manchester School* 48, (March): 39–62.

————. 1984. "Rational Expectations and the Theory of Macroeconomic Policy: An Exposition of Some of the Issues." *Journal of Economic Education* 15, (Winter): 55–69.

Urich, Thomas J., and Paul Wachtel. 1981. "Market Responses to the Weekly Money Supply Announcements in the 1970's." *Journal of Finance*. 36, (December): 1063–72.

von Furstenberg, G. 1983. "Changes in U.S. Interest Rates and Their Effects on European Interest and Exchange Rates." In *Exchange Rates and Trades Instability: Causes, Consequences and Remedies*, edited by D. Bigman and T. Tays. Cambridge, Mass.: Ballinger.

Walsh, C. E. 1984. "Interest Rate Volatility and Monetary Policy." *Journal of Money, Credit and Banking* 16, (May): 133–50.

Walters, A. 1971. "Consistent Expectations, Distributed Lags and the Quantity Theory." *Economic Journal* 81, (June): 273–81.

Westphal, U. 1983. "Comments on Domestic Savings and International Capital Movements in the Long Run and the Short Run." *European Economic Review* 21, (March/April): 157–59.

Zarnowitz, Victor. 1985. "Recent Work in Business Cycles in Historical Perspective." *Journal of Economic Literature* 23, (June): 523–80.

Index

ABOUT THE AUTHOR

GEORGE MACESICH is Professor of Economics and Director of the Center for Yugoslav-American Studies, Research, and Exchanges at the Florida State University in Tallahassee. He received his Ph.D. in economics from the University of Chicago. His books, among others, include *The International Monetary Economy and the Third World* (Praeger), *Monetarism: Theory and Policy, The Politics of Monetarism: Its Historical and Institutional Development, World Crisis and Developing Countries, Banking and Third World Debt: In Search of Solutions, World Banking and Finance: Cooperation Versus Conflict* (Praeger); *Economic Nationalism and Stability* (Praeger); with R. Lang and D. Vojnić, eds., *Essays on the Political Economy of Yugoslavia*; with Hui-Liang Tsai, *Money In Economic Systems;* with D. Dimitrijević, *Money and Finance in Yugoslavia: A Comparative Analysis* (Praeger).